TROLL

STUDENT
ATLAS

Library of Congress Cataloging-in-Publication Data

Dempsey, Michael W.
    Student atlas / by Michael Dempsey; revised by John C. Miles and
Constance Novis.
      p.   cm.
    Summary: Presents world and regional maps, a gazetteer, and
information about the earth's physical features.
    Includes gazetteer and index.
    ISBN 0-8167-2253-6 (lib. bdg.)   ISBN 0-8167-2254-4 (pbk.)
    1. Atlases. [1. Atlases.] I. Miles, John C. II. Novis,
Constance. III. Title.
G1021.D48 1991
912—dc20   90-675152

Published in the U.S.A. by Troll Associates, Inc.,
100 Corporate Drive, Mahwah, New Jersey.
Produced for Troll Associates, Inc., by
Joshua Morris Publishing Inc. in association
with Harper Collins.

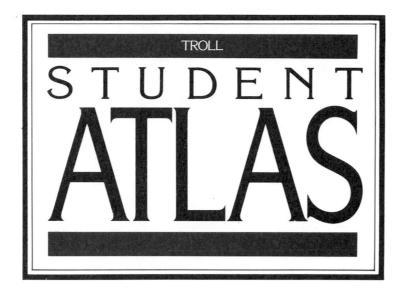

STUDENT ATLAS

TROLL

by
Michael Dempsey

Troll Associates

Contents

How to Use This Atlas

"Where is it?"

You've probably asked that question many times about unfamiliar places mentioned on TV and radio or in newspapers and magazines. Your Troll *Student Atlas* is meant to help you answer that question and many others about the world in which you live.

In its simplest form, an atlas is a book of maps. It is packed with facts and figures covering all parts of the globe. In our quickly changing world, there is a greater need than ever to understand its features.

Turn to the Gazetteer, a dictionary of world geography that is the largest section in the book. In alphabetical order, you'll find hundreds of places listed and briefly described, from "Aachen" to "Zurich." Here you'll learn where the Mississippi River starts and ends, how large a country Wales is, and what the main exports of Brazil are. Many of the entries are accompanied by full-color photographs and illustrations showing some important aspect of those places.

Toward the back of the book are two separate sections: "United States of America" and "Our World." These explain geography, climate, plant life, mountain ranges, industry, and population history, among other things.

Following those two sections are the maps and map index. In full color and carefully marked, the maps show major towns and geographical features. To find a particular place, first look in the map index for the page number. Then refer to the correct map.

A scale in both miles and kilometers is on each map. This scale will help you determine the distance between places. Boundaries between countries or states are marked with red lines, while rivers are marked with blue lines. Latitude and longitude are indicated by the horizontal and vertical blue lines crisscrossing the maps. The degrees of longitude and latitude are shown along the bottom and sides.

Deserts, mountains, and other land features are shaded in different colors for easy identification. Use the map key shown below to see which color goes with which terrain. Also listed are the symbols for capitals, cities of various sizes, and towns. The figures for mountain heights (above sea level) and underwater depths (below sea level) are provided, too.

You can use the Troll *Student Atlas* for study, school reports, or fun. It will satisfy your curiosity about places near and far, small and huge, isolated and densely populated. Keep it handy for quick reference.

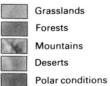

Grasslands	
Forests	
Mountains	
Deserts	
Polar conditions	

■ Cities with more than 1,000,000 people
● Cities with more than 250,000 people
• Towns
⊡ Country capital
▲ High peak, above sea level
▼ Depth, below sea level

A-Z Gazetteer of World Place Names

A

Aachen Industrial city in western Germany.

Aberdeen Port and city in Scotland.

Abidjan Port and capital city of Ivory Coast in Africa.

Abu Dhabi Capital city of United Arab Emirates.

Acapulco City and Pacific port in Mexico. It is a popular vacation resort.

Accra Port and capital city of Ghana.

Aconcagua Mountain in the Andes of western Argentina. It is the highest peak in South America. Height: 22,835 feet (6,965 meters).

Addis Ababa Capital city of Ethiopia.

Adelaide Port and capital city of South Australia, a state in Australia.

Aden Port and city of the Republic of Yemen.

Adriatic Sea Part of the Mediterranean Sea, along the east coast of Italy.

Aegean Sea Part of the Mediterranean Sea. It lies between Greece to the north and west, Turkey to the east, and Crete to the south.

Afghanistan Country in southwest Asia. Three quarters of the land is mountainous, with farmland in the valleys and plains. Wheat is the main crop. The leading exports are fruits, nuts, sheepskins, and hand-woven carpets. Area: 251,826 square miles (652,225 square kilometers). Capital: Kabul.

Africa The second-largest continent. It contains 53 countries. The largest is Sudan; the smallest is Seychelles. Africa's highest mountain is Mount Kilimanjaro, which stands 19,340 feet (5,899 meters) high. Its longest river is the Nile, which is 4,145 miles (6,680 kilometers) long. Area: 11,688,000 square miles (30,389,000 square kilometers).

Alabama One of the southern states in the United States, Alabama became the twenty-second U.S. state in 1819. Its economy was once mainly farming. Cotton, peanuts, soybeans, and wheat are the main crops, but manufacturing now dominates the economy. The chief industries are pulp and paper, chemicals, electronics, metal manufacturing, and textiles. Birmingham is the largest city and chief industrial center. Mobile is the chief port. Huntsville produces rockets and spacecraft. Area: 51,705 square miles (133,915 square kilometers). Capital: Montgomery.

Alaska The forty-ninth state of the United States. It was admitted to the Union in 1959. Alaska is the largest state and is located in northwest North America. It was nick-named "Seward's Folly" after U.S. Secretary of State William Seward bought the land from Russia for $7,200,000 in 1867. Gold was discovered in 1896. Minerals, especially oil, now dominate the economy. Fishing, forestry, and tourism are also important. Alaska has 8 national

A small island in the Aegean Sea.

A massive pipeline brings Alaska's oil to the Pacific, for shipping to her sister states.

parks. Area: 591,004 square miles (1,530,700 square kilometers). Capital: Juneau.

Albania Small, mountainous country on the Adriatic Sea. Albania is the poorest country in Europe despite considerable mineral resources. Area: 11,100 square miles (28,700 square kilometers). Capital: Tiranë.

Albany State capital of New York. Founded by Dutch settlers in 1624, it became the capital in 1797.

Alberta Western province of Canada. It has a thriving economy, producing about 90 percent of Canada's oil and natural gas, plus large quantities of coal. Beef and wheat are the chief agricultural products of the rich farmland in the southeast. The Rocky Mountains are in the southwest. Over 75 per-

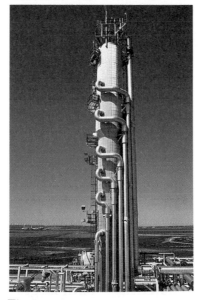

The gas and oil reserves of Alberta provide much of Canada's energy needs.

cent of the population lives in urban areas. The largest cities are Calgary and Edmonton. Area: 251,870 square miles (652,330 square kilometers). Capital: Edmonton.

Albuquerque City in the state of New Mexico. It is a popular mountain health resort.

Aleutian Islands Chain of islands in the Bering Sea that belong to the United States. Most of the islands are volcanic and mountainous.

Alexandria City and Mediterranean port in Egypt.

Algeria Second-largest country in Africa. Almost 90 percent of the land is desert. Most people live in the Mediterranean coastal plain where crops are grown. Area: 919,595 square miles (2,381,741 square kilometers). Capital: Algiers.

Algiers Port on the Mediterranean Sea and capital city of Algeria.

Alma-Ata U.S.S.R. city near Chinese border.

Almeria Mediterranean port and city in Spain.

Alps Mountain range in Europe. It stretches from the Riviera on the Mediterranean through Switzerland and Austria to Yugoslavia.

Amazon Longest river in South America and one of the two longest rivers in the world. It flows from the Andes mountains through Peru and Brazil to the Atlantic coast. Length: 4,000 miles (6,500 kilometers).

American Samoa Eight islands in the South Pacific Ocean that belong to the United States. Area: 77 square miles (200 square kilometers). Capital: Pago Pago.

Amiens City in northern France.

Amman Capital city of Jordan.

Amsterdam Port and capital city of the Netherlands.

Amur River in northeastern Asia. It flows between the U.S.S.R. and China. Length: 2,744 miles (4,418 kilometers).

Anchorage Major port and largest city in Alaska. Heavily damaged by an earthquake in 1964.

Andes Mountain system in South America. It runs along the Pacific coast for the entire length of the continent.

Andorra Small country in the Pyrenees Mountains between Spain and France. Area: 183 square miles (430 square kilometers). Capital: Andorra la Vella.

Angel Falls Waterfall on the Churun River, in southeast Venezuela. It is the highest falls in the world. Height: 3,200 feet (975 meters).

The Amstel River in Amsterdam.

An isolated village in the northern Andes.

Angers City in western France.

Angola Country in Africa. Area: 481,351 square miles (1,251,513 square kilometers). Capital: Luanda.

Ankara Capital city of Turkey.

Annapolis State capital of Maryland. Founded in 1649 by Puritans, the city has many historic buildings, including the U.S. Naval Academy.

Antananarivo Capital city of Madagascar.

Antarctica Fifth-largest continent. It is an icy region surrounding the South Pole that has no permanent population. Its highest mountain peak is Vinson Massif, which stands 16,864 feet (5,060 meters) high.

Antigua and Barbuda Small nation in the Caribbean Sea. It consists of three islands: Antigua, Barbuda, and tiny Redonda Island. Tourism is the main in-dustry. Area: 171 square miles (442 square kilometers). Capital: Saint John's.

Antwerp Port and city in Belgium.

Apennines Mountain range running along the length of Italy.

Appalachian Mountains North American mountain range. It runs from southern Quebec in Canada to Alabama, along the Atlantic coast.

Arabian Peninsula Desert land in southwestern Asia that is known for its large reserves of oil. It is separated from Africa by the Red Sea. The seven countries that lie on the peninsula are Saudi Arabia, Kuwait, Bahrain, Qatar, Oman, the Republic of Yemen, and United Arab Emirates.

Arabian Sea Part of the Indian Ocean between the Arabian Peninsula and India.

Aral Sea Inland body of

salt water in the southern U.S.S.R. It is fed by two rivers but has no outlet. Area: 25,659 square miles (64,000 square kilometers).

Ararat Highest mountain in Turkey. Height: 16,945 feet (5,165 meters).

Arctic Ocean Large body of water surrounding the North Pole. The Arctic Ocean is frozen over during winter. In summer much of the ice breaks up into icebergs. These drift southward, forming a hazard to shipping. Area: 3,662,000 square miles (9,485,100 square kilometers).

Arctic, The Region surrounding the North Pole. It contains the northern boundaries of the continents of North America, Europe, and Asia.

Argentina Second-largest country in South America. It is a major farming nation, exporting mostly agricultural products. Area: 1,073,400 square miles (2,780,092 square kilometers). Capital: Buenos Aires.

Arizona Sixth-largest state in the United States. Arizona became the forty-eighth state in 1912. Irrigation has turned its large desert areas into farmland. Livestock graze on higher ground. The Grand Canyon attracts many tourists. Area: 113,909 square miles (295,023 square kilometers).Capital: Phoenix.

Arkansas A southern state. It was acquired by the United States in 1803 as part of the Louisiana Purchase. It became the twenty-fifth state in 1836. Manufacturing and the farming of soybeans, rice, and chickens are important. Hot Springs National Park is a tourist attraction. Area: 53,104 square miles (137,539 square kilometers). Capital: Little Rock.

Arnhem City in the Netherlands.

Asia World's largest continent. It contains 42 countries. The largest (solely in Asia) is China; the smallest is the island country of Maldives. Asia's highest mountain is Mount Everest, which stands 29,028 feet (8,848 meters) high and is the world's highest point. Its longest river is the Yangtze. Area: 17,400,000 square miles (45,240,000 square kilometers).

Asia Minor Peninsula in western Asia. It lies between the Black Sea to the north, the Mediterranean Sea to the south, and the Aegean Sea to the west. Most of the peninsula is occupied by Turkey.

Astrakhan Port and city in the U.S.S.R.

Asuncion Port and capital city of Paraguay.

Aswan City in Egypt. Near the city is the large Aswan Dam.

Atacama Desert One of the world's driest deserts. It is located in northern Chile.

Athens Capital city of Greece.

Atlanta State capital of Georgia. It was originally named Terminus because it was the end of the Western and Atlantic Railroad. It has since become a major airline and commercial center.

Atlantic Ocean Second-largest ocean in the world. It lies between the American continents to the west and Europe and Africa to the east. Area: 31,814,640 square miles (82,700,000 square kilometers).

The beautiful monuments of ancient Athens sit atop the Acropolis.

The Auckland Bridge spans Waitemata Harbor on the eastern side of the city of Auckland, New Zealand.

Atlas Mountains Mountain system in northwest Africa.

Auckland Port and city in New Zealand.

Augusta State capital of Maine.

Austin State capital of Texas. It was named after Stephen Fuller Austin, a pioneer who founded it in the 1820s. It is a government and commercial center.

Australia Island continent and country. It is two-thirds desert or semi-desert. Most of the people live in the large coastal cities of Sydney, Melbourne, Brisbane, Adelaide, and Perth. The rest live in the fertile region along the eastern coastal plain. Australia is famous for its unique wildlife, such as the duck-billed platypus, kangaroo, wallaby, and koala. It is a major farming nation, exporting wool, wheat, dairy products, sugar cane, and meat. Mining and industry are also important. Australia is one of the world's most prosperous nations. Area: 2,967,909 square miles (7,686,000 square kilometers). Capital: Canberra.

Austria Country in central Europe. Almost three quarters of the land is mountainous. Wheat and corn are among the chief crops. Industry provides Austria's major exports. Tourism is also important. Area: 32,375 square miles (84,175 square kilometers). Capital: Vienna.

Avignon City in France.

Azores Group of volcanic islands. They lie in the northern Atlantic Ocean and belong to Portugal. Exports include fruit.

Australia's koala, an animal that lives in trees.

Australia's vast rural, remote area – the outback.

B

Baffin Bay Part of the North Atlantic Ocean between Greenland and Baffin Island, Canada. It is frozen for most of the year.

Baffin Island Island belonging to Canada. It lies mostly within the Arctic Circle.

Baghdad Capital city of Iraq.

Bahamas Country made up of about 3,000 coral islands and reefs. It is located southeast of Florida in the Atlantic Ocean. Only about 20 of the islands are inhabited. Tourism and banking are the chief industries. Area: 5,380 square miles (13,933 square kilometers). Capital: Nassau.

Bahrain Island country in the Persian Gulf. It has one of the Middle East's major oil refineries. Area: 264 square miles (685 square kilometers). Capital: Manama.

Baikal Huge lake in Siberia in the U.S.S.R. Area: 12,162 square miles (31,499 square kilometers).

Baja Peninsula Narrow arm of land in northwestern Mexico. It lies between the Gulf of California and the Pacific Ocean. It is made up of the Mexican states of Baja California Norte and Baja California Sur.

Baku Port and city in the U.S.S.R.

Balearic Islands Group of

Bangkok has hundreds of Buddhist temples. This row of bronze buddhas is in one of them.

islands in the Mediterranean Sea. They belong to Spain and include Majorca, Minorca, and Ibiza. The islands are a tourist resort.

Balkan Peninsula Land area in southeastern Europe. It includes Albania, Greece, Bulgaria, part of Turkey, and most of Yugoslavia.

Baltic Sea Large body of water in northern Europe. It lies between Sweden and the U.S.S.R.

Baltimore Port and city in Maryland. It has large steel, shipbuilding, and food processing industries. Francis Scott Key wrote "The Star-Spangled Banner" here.

Bamako Port and capital city of Mali.

Bandar Seri Begawan Capital city of Brunei.

Bangalore City in India.

Bangkok Capital city of Thailand.

Bangladesh Country in southern Asia. It is one of the poorest countries in the world. Nearly all the land is fertile and is

farmed, but it still cannot provide enough food for the population. Food is a major import. Area: 55,598 square miles (143,998 square kilometers). Capital: Dhaka.

Bangor City in Maine.

Bangui Port and capital city of the Central African Republic.

Banjul Port and capital city of Gambia.

Barbados Small, densely populated island nation in the Caribbean Sea. Its economy is based on sugar cane and tourism. Area: 166 square miles (430 square kilometers). Capital: Bridgetown.

Barcelona Port and city in Spain.

Barents Sea Part of the Arctic Ocean. It lies north of the U.S.S.R.

Bari Port and city in Italy.

Basel City in Switzerland.

Basra Port and city in Iraq.

Bath City in England.

Baton Rouge State capital of Louisiana. A port on the Mississippi River, it is noted for oil refining and food processing.

Beijing (also called Peking) Capital city of China. The inner city contains the old imperial palace.

Beira Port and city in Mozambique.

Beirut Port and capital city of Lebanon.

Belfast Port and capital city of Northern Ireland.

Belgium Country in western Europe. It is densely populated and highly industrialized. Manufactured goods, chemicals, and textiles are major exports. Three languages are spoken in Belgium: French, Dutch, and German. Area: 11,781 square miles (31,000 square kilometers). Capital: Brussels.

Low-lying northern Belgium is crisscrossed by rivers and canals.

Belgrade Port and capital city of Yugoslavia, on the Danube River.

Belize Small country on the Caribbean coast of Central America. Much of the land is covered by tropical rain forests. Area: 8,867 square miles (23,000 square kilometers). Capital: Belmopan.

Belmopan Capital city of Belize.

Bengal, Bay of Part of the Indian Ocean. It lies between the east coast of India and the west coast of Burma.

Benghazi Port and city in Libya.

Benin Small, densely populated country in western Africa. Palm oil, raw cotton, and coffee are major exports. Area: 43,483 square miles (113,000 square kilometers). Capital: Porto-Novo.

Bering Sea Part of the northern Pacific Ocean between Siberia in the U.S.S.R. and Alaska.

Bering Strait Stretch of water connecting the Arctic Ocean with the Pacific Ocean. It separates North America and Asia.

Berlin City in eastern Germany. After World War II, the city was divided into two parts. East Berlin became the capital of the German Democratic Republic (East Germany). West Berlin formed close ties with the Federal Republic of Germany (West Germany). The Berlin Wall was built in 1961

Bern's medieval clock tower. When the hour strikes, out come a mechanized man on a horse, a man in armor, a rooster, and dancing bears.

because of conflicts between the two sides. The year 1989 began a period of great changes, and steps were taken to remove the wall dividing the city.

Bermuda Group of islands in the western Atlantic Ocean. A British colony, it has a large tourist industry. Area: 20 square miles (53 square kilometers). Capital: Hamilton.

Bern Capital city of Switzerland.

Bethlehem Town in Jordan. It is believed to be the birthplace of Jesus.

Bhopal City in central India.

Bhutan Small country in southern Asia. It has close ties with India. Most of its people are farmers. Area: 17,950 square miles (46,500 square kilometers). Capital: Thimphu.

Bilbao Port and city in Spain.

Birmingham City in Alabama. A major industrial center, it is in a rich iron ore region.

Birmingham City in England. It is a major manufacturing center.

Biscay, Bay of Part of the Atlantic Ocean. It is bounded by Spain and France.

Bismarck State capital of North Dakota. First settled in 1872, it became the state capital in 1889.

Bissau Port and seat of government of Guinea-Bissau in Africa.

Blackpool City in England.

Black Sea Body of water surrounded by the U.S.S.R., Asia Minor, and the Balkan Peninsula. Area: 175,000 square miles (453,000 square kilometers).

Bloemfontein Judicial capital city of South Africa.

Bogota Capital city of Colombia.

Boise State capital of Idaho. The largest city in the state, it is a trade and transportation center.

Bolivia Country in South America. More than half of the people are farmers who grow only enough food for their own families. Their main crops are corn and potatoes. Cash crops include sugar cane and coffee. Large oil and gas deposits have been discovered. Area: 424,162 square miles (1,089,000 square kilometers). Capitals: Sucre (legal) and La Paz (administrative).

Bologna City in Italy.

Bombay Port and city in India.

Bonn City in western Germany, on the Rhine River.

Bordeaux Port and city in France.

Borneo Third-largest island in the world. It contains Brunei and parts of Malaysia and the Republic of Indonesia.

Boston State capital of Massachusetts. It is a major port and the commercial center of New England. It was the site of the Boston Tea Party in 1773.

Bothnia, Gulf of Shallow part of the Baltic Sea. It lies between Finland and Sweden.

Botswana Country in Africa. It consists of mostly scrub land suitable for cattle ranching. Swampland in the northwest is rich in wildlife and is a popular tourist attraction. Area: 224,607 square miles (581,730 square kilometers). Capital: Gaborone.

Brahmaputra River River flowing through Tibet, India, and Bangladesh. Length: 1,680 miles (2,704 kilometers).

Brasilia Capital city of Brazil.

Bratislava City in Czechoslovakia.

A field hand works among the coffee plants in Brazil.

Brazil Fifth-largest country in the world. It occupies almost half of South America. In the north, dense forest covers half the country. Most people live in the southeast. Brazil exports coffee, cocoa, sugar cane, and tobacco as well as industrial products. It has important mineral deposits. Area: 3,286,487 square miles (8,511,965 square kilometers). Capital: Brasilia.

Brazzaville Port and capital city of Congo.

Brescia City in Italy.

Brighton City in England.

Brisbane Port and city in Australia.

The city of Brisbane, seen from the Brisbane River.

British Columbia Province of Canada. Located on the country's west coast, it became a province in 1871. Its natural resources include timber, copper, oil, coal, and fish. The largest city and main seaport is Vancouver. Area: 366,255 square miles (947,000 square kilometers). Capital: Victoria.

Bruges City in Belgium.

Brunei Small, oil-rich nation in Asia. It is located on the island of Borneo. Area: 2,226 square miles (5,800 square kilometers). Capital: Bandar Seri Begawan.

Brussels Capital city of Belgium.

Bucharest Capital city of Romania.

Budapest Capital city of Hungary.

Buenos Aires Capital city and leading port of Argentina.

Buffalo Port and industrial city in New York State.

Bujumbura Capital city of Burundi.

Bulgaria Country in Europe. Its main crops are wheat and corn. Machinery is an important export. Area: 42,823 square miles (111,000 square kilometers). Capital: Sofia.

Burgos City in Spain.

Burkina Faso Country in Africa. It is bordered by the Sahara and sometimes receives no rain for years. The people live by keeping livestock and farming.

Timber is one of British Columbia's–and Canada's– leading products.

Area: 105,869 square miles (274,179 square kilometers). Capital: Ouagadougou.

Burma Country in southeastern Asia. Rice is the main crop and leading export, along with teakwood. Burma produces some oil and also has many mineral deposits. Area: 261,218 square miles (676,552 square kilometers. Capital: Rangoon.

Burundi Nation in the center of Africa. Coffee is the major export. Area: 10,759 square miles (28,000 square kilometers). Capital: Bujumbura.

Bute Island of southwest Scotland. It lies in the Firth of Clyde, an Atlantic inlet.

C

Cadiz Port and city in Spain.

Caen City in France.

Cairo Capital city of Egypt. It is located on the Nile River.

Calcutta One of the largest cities in India and its most active port.

Calgary City in Alberta, Canada.

The annual Calgary Stampede includes rodeos, horse racing, and a livestock show.

California Third-largest state in size and the most populated state in the United States. The discovery of gold in 1848 led to rapid settlement. California became the thirty-first state in 1850. The best farmland is in the irrigated Central Valley. Farm produce includes beef, dairy products, eggs and poultry, cereals, and grapes and other fruits and vegetables. California is the third-largest oil producer in the country. Many other minerals are also mined. The economy is dominated by manufacturing. The scenic coast, several national parks, and two of the nation's most famous cities, Los Angeles and San Francisco, draw many tourists to California. Area: 158,693 square miles (411,103 square kilometers). Capital: Sacramento.

Cambridge City in England.

Cameroon Country in Africa. The economy is based on agriculture. Crops include cocoa, coffee, peanuts, bananas, and cotton, which are all exported. Area: 183,591 square miles (475,000 square kilometers). Capital: Yaounde.

Canada Second-largest country in the world. Canada has one of the highest standards of living in the world. Much of the land is interior lowlands, bordered on the west by the Rocky Mountains. In the north lie a large group of islands and the Arctic Ocean. Most of the people live in the southeast in the lowlands bordering the Great Lakes. Canada's natural resources include large oil and gas deposits. To the north of the southern farming regions are huge forests of evergreens. Lumber, steel, aluminum, paper, machinery, cars, and high-technology products are major exports. Minerals include copper, nickel, and zinc.

The settlement of Canada was begun by the French. Anglo-French wars resulted in the colony passing to British rule in 1763. After union of the provinces in 1867, settlement expanded rapidly westward. In 1931, Canada became an independent member of the British Commonwealth. Control over Canada's constitution was transferred from Britain to Canada in 1982. Area: 3,849,674 square miles (9,970,610 square kilometers). Capital: Ottawa.

A local market in Cameroon, Africa.

Canary Islands Group of islands in the Atlantic belonging to Spain.

Canberra Capital city of Australia.

Cannes Port and city in France.

Canterbury City in England.

Canton Port and city in China.

Cape Town Legislative capital city of South Africa.

Cape Verde Country in the Atlantic Ocean off the coast of Africa. The economy is based on farming and fishing. Area: 1,557 square miles (4,030 square kilometers). Capital: Praia.

Caracas Capital city of Venezuela.

Cardiff Capital city of Wales.

Caribbean Sea Part of the Atlantic Ocean. It is bounded by the West Indies, Central America, and northern South America.

Caroline Islands Group of islands in the western Pacific Ocean. They are part of the United States Trust Territory of the Pacific Islands.

Caroni River River in Venezuela.

Carson City State capital of Nevada.

Casablanca Port and city in Morocco.

Caspian Sea Inland sea surrounded by Iran and the U.S.S.R. Area: 143,630 square miles (372,000 square kilometers).

Caucasus Mountain range in the U.S.S.R.

Cayenne Capital city of French Guiana.

Cayman Islands Three islands in the Caribbean Sea belonging to Great Britain. Capital: Georgetown.

Central African Republic Country in central Africa. It has few resources and a small population. Most people are farmers. Diamonds are the chief export. Area: 240,535 square miles (622,984 square kilometers). Capital: Bangui.

Central America Land link between the United States and South America. It contains Belize, Guatemala, Honduras, El Salvador, Nicaragua, Costa Rica, and Panama.

Bull riding at Cheyenne, Wyoming.

Chad Country in central Africa. It is one of the least developed nations in the world. Most people raise crops for their own families; others are nomadic herders. Area: 495,752 square miles (1,283,901 square kilometers). Capital: N'Djamena.

Changchung City in China.

Changsha City in China.

Channel Islands Group of self-governing islands in the English Channel.

Charleston Capital of West Virginia. Capital since 1885, Charleston is a transport and trade center.

Charlotte City in North Carolina.

Charlottetown Capital city of the province of Prince Edward Island, Canada.

Chengdu City in China.

Chernobyl City in the U.S.S.R. In 1986, a serious accident at a nuclear power plant in Chernobyl drew worldwide attention to the city.

Cheyenne State capital of Wyoming. Founded in 1867, the city is named after the Cheyenne Indian tribe.

Chicago One of the largest cities in the United States. It is located in Illinois on the southwestern shore of Lake Michigan. It is an important port and a major industrial and commercial center. It has one of the busiest airports in the world.

Chile Country on the southwest coast of South America. The majority of the people live in the central region, which is suitable for agriculture. Chile is rich in minerals, producing copper, iron ore, coal, and petroleum. Area: 292,257 square miles (756,900 square kilometers). Capital: Santiago.

A quarter of all goods within China are transported by water.

China Third-largest country in the world. It has about 20 percent of the world's population. In the 1970s, China opened its doors to Western trade and tourists. Rice is the chief cereal crop in the south; wheat and millet are grown in the north. Other important crops are sugar cane, soybeans, cotton, and corn. China has huge coal deposits, natural gas, petroleum, iron ore, and tungsten. Leading manufactured products are steel, textiles, machinery, and chemicals. One of the world's earliest civilizations was established in China. Area: 3,678,470 square miles (9,527,200 square kilometers). Capital: Beijing (Peking).

Chongqing Port in China.

Christchurch City in New Zealand.

Christmas Island Coral island in the Pacific Ocean. It is also called Kiritimati Atoll.

Churun River in Venezuela.

Cincinnati Port and industrial city in Ohio.

Ciudad Juarez City in Mexico on the border of the United States.

Cologne City in western Germany.

Colombia Country in South America. It has coastline on both the Pacific Ocean and the Caribbean Sea. Many of the people are farmers. Coffee, sugar cane, and cotton are important plantation crops. Gold, platinum, and emeralds are also mined. Area: 439,735 square miles (1,138,825 square kilometers). Capital: Bogota.

Colombo Port and capital city of Sri Lanka.

Colorado One of the Rocky Mountain states.

Colorado was admitted to the United States in 1876 as the thirty-eighth state. Irrigated farms produce wheat, corn, and sugar beets. Colorado also has large herds of cattle and sheep. In the 1800s, mining helped make Colorado prosperous, but manufacturing is now the chief activity. Computers, machinery, and metal goods are important products. Tourism, including winter sports, is also important. Area: 104,247 square miles (269,998 square kilometers). Capital: Denver.

Colorado River River flowing through the southwestern United States and Mexico. It passes through many canyons, including the Grand Canyon. The Colorado River is used extensively for irrigation and has numerous dams, including the famous Hoover Dam. Length: 1,450 miles (2,330 kilometers).

Columbia State capital of South Carolina. The capital since 1786, it is a commercial and university center.

Columbus State capital of Ohio.

Comoros Island nation in the Indian Ocean. Vanilla, coconuts, and cocoa are the chief exports. Area: 838 square miles (2,171 square kilometers). Capital: Moroni.

Conakry Port and capital city of Guinea.

Concord State capital of New Hampshire. The city has been the capital since 1808.

Congo Country in Africa. It is located on the equator and has a short Atlantic coastline. Most of the people depend on agriculture for their livelihood. Area: 132,047 square miles (342,000 square kilometers). Capital: Brazzaville.

Congo River in Africa. Length: 2,900 miles (4,667 kilometers).

Connecticut One of the original 13 states in the United States. Connecticut ratified the Constitution on January 9, 1788, to become the fifth state. It is a major manufacturing state. Products include transport equipment, machinery, and metal goods. Farmers produce milk, eggs and poultry, tobacco, and other items. Its coastline has popular summer resorts. Area: 5,009 square miles (12,973 square kilometers). Capital: Hartford.

Cook Islands Group of islands in the South Pacific Ocean.

Copenhagen Port and capital city of Denmark. It is an important commercial center.

Coral Sea Part of the Pacific Ocean, northeast of Australia.

Cordoba City in Spain.

Corfu Island off the northwest mainland coast of Greece.

Cork City in the Republic of Ireland.

Corsica Large island in the Mediterranean Sea and part of France.

Costa Rica Central American country. Coffee and bananas are the chief cash crops and major exports. Area: 19,652 square miles (50,000 square kilometers). Capital: San Jose.

Crete Largest of the Greek Mediterranean islands.

Cuba Island country in the Caribbean Sea. The primary cash crops are sugar and tobacco. Mineral resources include nickel, iron, manganese, chromium, and copper. In 1959, following a rebellion, it became a Communist state. Area: 44,218 square miles (115,000 square kilometers). Capital: Havana.

Cyprus Island country in the Mediterranean Sea off the coast of Turkey. Crops include grapes, wheat, and citrus fruits.

A fishing harbor on the coast of Corsica.

Area: 3,572 square miles. (9,250 square kilometers). Capital: Nicosia.

Czechoslovakia Country in Europe. Although farming is important, the nation is highly industrialized. Products include iron and steel, military equipment, cars, machinery, textiles, and chemicals. Area: 49,371 square miles (127,900 square kilometers). Capital: Prague.

In the countryside of Cyprus, a horse and cart are often used for transportation.

D

Dakar Port and capital city of Senegal.

Dallas City in Texas. It is a major commerce center.

Damascus Capital city of Syria. It is said to be the oldest city in the world.

Danube Second-largest river in Europe. It flows from southwestern Germany east to the Black Sea. Length: 1,770 miles (2,850 kilometers).

Dardanelles Narrow body of water. It connects the Sea of Marmara with the Aegean Sea.

Dar es Salaam Port and capital city of Tanzania.

Darwin Port and city in Australia.

Davis Strait Narrow body of water. It connects Baffin Bay with the Atlantic Ocean.

Dead Sea Large saltwater lake. It is bordered by Israel and Jordan. It has a very high salt and mineral content.

Delaware The first of the original thirteen states in the United States. Delaware ratified the Constitution on December 7, 1787. The second-smallest state, Delaware is mostly flat with a long coastline facing the Atlantic Ocean. Poultry raising and farming are important, but manufacturing is the main activity. The chief products are chemicals, food, and paper products. Area: 2,044 square miles (5,295 square kilometers). Capital: Dover.

Denmark European country. It consists of the peninsula of Jutland and a number of islands, the largest of which are Zealand and Fyn. Denmark specializes in dairy and pig farming. There are few mineral resources. Light industries, such as the manufacture of electronic equipment, textiles, and furniture, are important. Area: 16,615 square miles (43,000 square kilometers). Capital: Copenhagen.

Denver State capital of Colorado. Founded by gold miners in 1858, it was named after J.W. Denver, the governor of the Kansas territory. At that time, the territory included Denver. The city owes its development to the mineral wealth of the Rocky Mountains. It is a popular skiing and tourist center.

Des Moines Capital of Iowa. It is also the largest city in the state.

Detroit City in Michigan. It is the center of the automobile industry in the United States.

Dhaka Capital city of Bangladesh.

Dijon City in France.

District of Columbia (D.C.) Federal district of the United States. It is located between Maryland and Virginia. It contains the city of Washington. The District was established in 1791. The federal government moved there in 1800.

Djibouti Country in Africa. It is barren and has no mineral resources. The city of Djibouti is an important port. Area: 8,410 square miles (21,783 square kilometers). Capital: Djibouti.

Doha Port and capital city of Qatar.

Dominica Mountainous island country in the Caribbean Sea. It became independent in

Dead Sea.

1978. The climate and scenery have made tourism a valuable industry. Bananas and coconuts are the chief exports. Area: 290 square miles (750 square kilometers). Capital: Roseau.

Dominican Republic Caribbean country. It occupies the eastern part of the island of Hispaniola. Most of the people are farmers, and the standard of living is low. The chief cash crop is sugar. Sugar refining is the chief industry. Area: 18,704 square miles (49,000 square kilometers). Capital: Santo Domingo.

Don River in the U.S.S.R. Length: 1,224 miles (2,000 kilometers).

Dover State capital of Delaware. Capital since 1777, Dover is a university and agricultural center.

Dover Port and city on the south coast of England.

Dover, Strait of Narrow body of water. It connects the English Channel with the North Sea, between southern England and France.

Dresden Large city in eastern Germany. It is famous for its fine china.

Dubai Port and city in the United Arab Emirates. It is located on the Persian Gulf.

Dublin Capital city of the Republic of Ireland. It is also a port on the Irish Sea.

Dundee Port and city in Scotland.

E

East China Sea Part of the Pacific Ocean. It is located between China and the southern islands of Japan.

Easter Island Volcanic island in the South Pacific Ocean. It is located off the coast of Chile.

East London Port and city in South Africa.

East Siberian Sea Part of the Arctic Ocean. It is located off the northern coast of the eastern U.S.S.R.

Ecuador Country in South America. The country has fertile plains between its coast and the Andes mountains. Earthquakes are frequent. Ecuador has valuable petroleum reserves, and most of the nation's wealth comes from selling oil. Area: 109,484 square miles (283,561 square kilometers). Capital: Quito.

Edinburgh Capital city of Scotland.

Edmonton Capital city of the province of Alberta, Canada. It is the center of an oil-producing region.

Egypt Country in northern Africa. It has a hot climate. Except for the fertile valley of the Nile

Indians in their traditional felt hats and ponchos are a common sight in the street markets of Ecuador.

Colossal statues from the temple of Abu Simbel in Egypt.

River, most of the country is desert. Crops include cotton, sugar cane, dates, fruit, and vegetables. Tourism is important, with many visitors coming to admire the Pyramids and other ancient wonders. Area: 386,000 square miles (1,001,710 square kilometers). Capital: Cairo.

Elbe River in Europe. It flows from Czechoslovakia to the North Sea. Length: 720 miles (1,160 kilometers).

Elbrus Mountain in the U.S.S.R. Standing 18,480 feet (5,630 meters) high, it is located in the Caucasus mountain range.

El Paso City in Texas. Located on the Mexican border, it is an important port of entry into the United States.

El Salvador Small country in Central America. The economy is based on agriculture. Coffee, cotton, and sugar are the main cash crops and exports. Area: 8,260 square miles (21,400 square kilometers). Capital: San Salvador.

England Part of the United Kingdom. It is the most densely populated part of the U.K.,with the largest cities. These include London. Tourists visit England to see its historic towns, castles, and scenery. Its wealth comes mostly from business activities, such as banking, insurance, trade, and industry. Area: 50,331 square miles (130,000 square kilometers). Capital: London.

English Channel Narrow body of water. It connects the North Sea with the Atlantic Ocean, between England and France.

Entebbe City in Uganda.

Equatorial Guinea Country in Africa. It is made up of a small, forested mainland area and a number of offshore islands. The economy is based on agriculture, particularly cocoa and coffee. Area: 10,832 square miles (28,000 square kilometers). Capital: Malabo.

Erie, Lake Shallowest lake of the five Great Lakes. Lake Erie covers an area of 9,910 square miles (25,667 square kilometers). The American-Canadian border passes through the center of the lake.

Esfahan City in Iran.

Ethiopia Country in Africa. It is a land of hot deserts and cool plateaus. Some forest exists. Vegetation is mainly scrub, dying off in the dry season and springing up again when the rains come. Many people live by farming and raising livestock. The chief cash crop is coffee. Area: 471,778 square miles (1,221,900 square kilometers). Capital: Addis Ababa.

Etna, Mount Active volcano in Italy. It is the highest active volcano in Europe. It has erupted at least 140 times.

Euphrates River in southwest Asia. It flows from eastern Turkey, through Syria and Iraq, into the Persian Gulf. Length: 1,700 miles (2,736 kilometers).

Europe Sixth-largest continent. It has over 30 countries, including part of the U.S.S.R., the world's largest country, and Vatican City, the world's smallest country. Europe's highest mountain is Mount Elbrus, which stands 18,480 feet (5,630 meters) high. Its longest river is the 2,293-mile-long (3,700-kilometer-long) Volga. Area: 4,065,000 square miles (10,528,000 square kilometers).

Everest, Mount Highest mountain in the world. It is in the Himalaya range, on the boundary between Tibet and Nepal. It was first climbed in 1953. Height: 29,028 feet (8,848 meters).

Everglades Large subtropical area of lakes, marshes, and swamps in Florida. One section is a national park, with mangrove swamps and many rare animals and plants.

F

Faeroe Islands Group of islands belonging to Denmark in the North Atlantic Ocean. They are located between Iceland and the Shetland Islands.

Falkland Islands Group of islands belonging to the United Kingdom in the South Atlantic Ocean. They are located near the southern tip of South America.

Fez City in Morocco.

Fiji Country containing over 800 islands in the southwest Pacific Ocean. The mainstay of the economy is sugar production and tourism. Area: 7,000 square miles (18,000 square kilometers). Capital: Suva.

Finland Country in Europe. It is covered mostly by lakes and forests. Less than one tenth of the land is used for growing crops. Timber, pulp, and paper products are the mainstay of the economy. Other industries include shipbuilding, textiles, and glassware. Area: 130,119 square miles (337,000 square kilometers). Capital: Helsinki.

Finland, Gulf of Part of the Baltic Sea between Finland and the U.S.S.R.

Florence City in Italy.

Florida A southern state in the United States. Florida is the home of many retired Americans. It receives about 40 million tourists a year. Miami Beach is one of several famous seaside resorts. Other attractions include Disney World near Orlando, the Everglades National Park, and the Kennedy Space Center at Cape Canaveral. Florida was mostly under Spanish rule from the 16th century until 1819, when it was ceded to the United States. Florida became the twenty-seventh state in 1845. Industrial products include electrical machinery and equipment. Fruits and nuts, sugar, beef, and dairy foods are major farm products. Area: 58,560 square miles (151,670 square kilometers). Capital: Tallahassee.

Fortaleza Port and city in Brazil.

Fort Worth City in Texas. Livestock and oil refining are important to its economy.

France Country in Europe. It has coasts on the Atlantic Ocean, the English Channel, and the Mediterranean Sea. The climate is cool or temperate apart from

Lakes and forests cover much of Finland. In the north, they give way to bare tundra wastes.

Mount Fuji in Japan.

G

Gabon Country in Africa. It is mostly covered by rain forest. Most people farm the land, but forestry and petroleum production are the main industries. Area: 103,347 square miles (267,667 square kilometers). Capital: Libreville.

Gaborone Capital city of Botswana.

Galapagos Islands Group of islands in the Pacific Ocean, known for their unique wildlife.

Gambia Country in Africa. Its economy is based on agriculture. Area: 4,361 square miles (11,295 square kilometers). Capital: Banjul.

Ganges River in Asia. It flows through India and Bangladesh. Length: 1,557 miles (2,400 kilometers).

Gdansk Port and industrial city in Poland.

Geneva City in Switzerland. It is located on Lake Geneva.

Genoa Port and city in Italy. It is the birthplace of Christopher Columbus.

Georgetown Port and capital city of Guyana.

Georgia Fourth state to join the United States in 1788. The economy is based on textiles, food products, transport equipment, and timber products. Farming is important. Area: 58,876 square miles (152,488 square kilometers). Capital: Atlanta.

the hot Mediterranean southeast and the cold mountain regions. The main industries include car and aircraft manufacturing. Many people are involved in farming. France is known for its world-famous wines. Area: 211,208 square miles (547,026 square kilometers). Capital: Paris.

Frankfort State capital of Kentucky. It has been the capital since 1792.

Frankfurt City in western Germany.

Franz Josef Land Group of islands in the Arctic Ocean. They were claimed by the U.S.S.R. in 1926.

Fredericton Capital city of the province of New Brunswick, Canada.

Freetown Port and capital city of Sierra Leone.

French Guiana Country in South America. It is under French control. Sugar cane is the chief cash crop. Gold and iron ore are among the chief minerals. Area: 35,135 square miles (91,000 square kilometers). Capital: Cayenne.

Frunze City in the U.S.S.R.

Fuji, Mount Inactive volcanic mountain. It is the highest peak in Japan. Height: 12,388 feet (3,776 meters).

Fushun City in China.

Fuzhou City in China.

Flowing through western Germany is the Rhine, Europe's greatest river.

Germany Country in Europe. In 1949, it was divided into two nations, East and West Germany. In 1989, steps were taken to reunify the country. Manufacturing is important to the economy. The Ruhr and other industrial areas produce iron, steel, and other metal goods, precision instruments, chemicals, and electronics. Germany is among the world leaders in automobile making. Crops and livestock are raised on small farms, but Germany still has to import food. Area: 137,773 square miles (358,210 square kilometers).

Ghana Country in Africa. The climate is hot with much rainfall in the south, where many people live. The chief agricultural export is cocoa. Lumbering, fishing, and manufacturing are also important. Area: 92,100 square miles (238,598 square kilometers). Capital: Accra.

Ghent Port and city in Belgium.

Gibraltar Peninsula with a 1,396-foot-high (426-meter-high) rock in the center. The peninsula, which belongs to Great Britain, juts out from Spain at the entrance of the Mediterranean Sea. Area: 2.25 square miles (6 square kilometers).

Gibraltar, Strait of Narrow body of water between Spain and Morocco. It connects the Mediterranean Sea with the Atlantic Ocean.

Glasgow City in Scotland.

Gobi Vast desert region. It is located in Mongolia and China. Area: about 500,000 square miles (1,300,000 square kilometers).

Good Hope, Cape of Point of land at the southern tip of Africa.

Goteborg Port and city in Sweden.

Granada City in southern Spain.

Grand Canyon An enormously deep and wide canyon in northwest Arizona. It is one of the world's natural wonders. Cut by the Colorado River, the canyon is over a mile deep and varies in width from 4 to 18 miles (6 to 30 kilometers). Spectacular color changes occur as the sunlight strikes the multicolored, banded rock layers. Its beauty makes it a major tourist attraction.

Graz City in Austria.

The Grand Canyon of the Colorado River, Arizona.

The Great Barrier Reef, with its corals and colorful tropical fish.

Great Barrier Reef Coral reef off the coast of Australia.

Great Britain Island country in northwestern Europe. It contains England, Scotland, and Wales. (Great Britain and Northern Ireland together form the United Kingdom. Sometimes "Great Britain" and "United Kingdom" are loosely used for each other.) Separated from the European continent by the English Channel, Great Britain is a land of rolling fields and meadows. Its chief products include barley, cattle, oats, chemicals, and clothing. Area: 88,798 square miles (230,875 square kilometers). Capital: London.

Great Dividing Range Mountain range in eastern Australia. It runs almost the entire length of the continent.

Great Lakes Group of five large lakes in North America. They are named Superior, Michigan, Ontario, Huron, and Erie. The lakes are interconnected and linked to the Atlantic Ocean by the Saint Lawrence River.

Great Salt Lake Inland sea in northwestern Utah. It is considered a natural wonder of the world. Area: 2,328 square miles (6,029 square kilometers).

Greece Country in Europe. Located on the Mediterranean coast, it consists of a mainland plus many islands. The ruins of ancient Greece and the warm, sunny climate make Greece a popular tourist resort. Most Greek people live by farming. They grow grapes and other fruits, olives, tobacco, and wheat. Others live by fishing. Area: 50,944 square miles (131,979 square kilometers). Capital: Athens.

Greenland Large island lying mostly in the Arctic Circle. It is a province of Denmark. Greenland is inhabited mainly in coastal settlements. It has important mineral deposits. Some of the island is permanently covered with ice. Area: 839,999 square miles (2,175,600 square kilometers). Capital: Godthab.

Grenada Island country in the Caribbean Sea. It is one of the smallest countries in the world. Its economy is based on agriculture and tourism. Area: 133 square miles (344 square kilometers). Capital: Saint George's.

Grenoble City in France.

Guadalajara City in western Mexico.

Guadeloupe Two islands belonging to France in the Caribbean Sea. Capital: Basse-Terre.

Guam Island territory of the United States in the Pacific Ocean. It has important military bases.

A Guam islander demonstrates the traditional skills of salt making.

Guatemala Country in Central America. Its economy is based on agriculture. Coffee is an important cash crop and accounts for about half the country's exports. Area: 42,042 square miles (109,000 square kilometers). Capital: Guatemala City.

Guatemala City Capital city of Guatemala. It was badly damaged by an earthquake in 1976.

Guayaquil Port and city in Ecuador.

Guinea Country in Africa. It has mineral deposits of bauxite and iron ore. Coffee, bananas, and pineapples are the main agricultural exports. Area: 94,925 square miles (246,000 square kilometers). Capital: Conakry.

Guinea-Bissau Country in Africa. Its economy is based on rice, peanuts, and cattle farming. Area: 13,948 square miles (36,000 square kilometers). Capital: Bissau.

Gulf of Mexico Arm of the Atlantic Ocean off the east coast of Mexico.

Gumti River of northern India. It flows 500 miles (805 kilometres) to the Ganges.

Guyana Country in northern South America on the Atlantic. Its population is concentrated in the northern coastal region. The inland area is densely forested. Sugar and the mineral bauxite make up the main exports. Area: 83,000 square miles (215,000 square kilometers). Capital: Georgetown.

H

Hague, The City and seat of government of The Netherlands.

Haifa Port and city in Israel.

Haiti Country in the Caribbean Sea, on the island of Hispaniola. The economy is mostly agricultural, and coffee is exported. Manufacturing is also important. Area: 10,714 square miles (27,750 square kilometers). Capital: Port-au-Prince.

Halifax Port and capital city of Nova Scotia, Canada.

Hamburg Port and city in northern Germany.

Hamilton Port and city in Ontario, Canada.

Hannover City in northern Germany.

Hanoi Port and capital city of Vietnam.

Harare Capital city of Zimbabwe.

Harbin City in China.

Harrisburg State capital of Pennsylvania. Its economy is based on steel, textiles, printing, and machinery.

Hartford State capital of Connecticut. Founded in 1636 by the Dutch, the city is noted for its large number of insurance companies.

Havana Port and capital city of Cuba.

Hawaii Group of about 130 volcanic islands in the central Pacific Ocean. Hawaii became the fiftieth state in the United States in 1959. The inhabited islands are Hawaii (the "Big Island"), Maui, Oahu (where Honolulu is located), Kauai, Molokai, Lanai, and Niihau. Tourism is a major activity. Processed foods are the chief products. Sugar, pineapples, and coffee are also produced. Area: 6,450 square miles (16,705 square kilometers). Capital: Honolulu.

Hebrides Group of islands off the west coast of Scotland.

Heidelberg City in southwestern Germany.

Helena State capital of Montana. It was founded in 1864 when gold was discovered there.

Helsinki Port and capital city of Finland.

Himalayas Mountain system in central Asia.

Hiroshima City in Japan. It was largely destroyed

Kilauea Volcano, Hawaii.

Hong Kong at night.

in 1945 by an atomic bomb explosion, but later rebuilt.

Hispaniola Island in the West Indies. It contains the Republic of Haiti and the Dominican Republic. Area: 29,420 square miles (76,200 square kilometers).

Hobart Port and capital city of Tasmania, Australia.

Ho Chi Minh City Port and city in Vietnam.

Honduras Country in Central America. It has a mild climate, except on its tropical coast. Its economy is based on agriculture. Area: 43,277 square miles (112,000 square kilometers). Capital: Tegucigalpa.

Hong Kong British colony in Asia. It is one of the busiest ports in the world. Area: 400 square miles (1,000 square kilometers).

Honolulu State capital of Hawaii. Located on Oahu Island, it is a major port and has an important international airport.

Hormuz, Strait of Water link between the Gulf of Oman and the Persian Gulf in southwestern Asia.

Horn, Cape Most southerly point of South America.

Houston Port and city in Texas. It is the center of a rich oil and gas producing region. It is also the site of NASA's manned spacecraft center.

Huang He River in China. It is also known as the Yellow River. Length: 2,900 miles (4,700 kilometers).

Hudson Bay Inland sea in northwestern Canada. Area: 316,500 square miles (819,730 square kilometers).

Hungary Country in Europe. It exports grains, meat, and vegetables. Manufacturing is very important, even though raw materials have to be imported. Area: 35,921 square miles (93,000 square kilometers). Capital: Budapest.

Huron, Lake Second-largest of the Great Lakes. It covers an area of 23,010 square miles (59,570 square kilometers).

Hyderabad City in India.

The sixteenth-century Char Minar Gate stands at the center of the old city of Hyderabad in India.

I

Iceland Island country in the North Atlantic Ocean. Much of it is covered with large ice fields. Less than one percent of the land can grow crops. The economy is based on fishing, exporting fish products, and some sheep farming. Area: 39,769 square miles (103,000 square kilometers). Capital: Reykjavik.

Idaho A Rocky Mountain state. It became the forty-third state in the United States in 1890. Idaho had a gold rush in the 1860s. The leading industry today is farming, with potatoes as the best-known product. Wheat, hay, and barley are grown. Idaho produces silver and manufactures food products and machinery. Area: 83,557 square miles (216,412 square kilometers). Capital: Boise.

Illinois A midwestern state. In 1818 it became the twenty-first state. Fertile prairies make farming important. A leading activity is manufacturing, especially around Chicago. Area: 56,400 square miles (146,075 square kilometers). Capital: Springfield.

Inchon City and port in South Korea.

India Country in Asia. It has the second-largest population in the world. Many Indians still live in small villages. Crops grown include rice, cereals, cotton, sugar cane, and tea. India has coal and other minerals. Industry is developing rapidly. Area: 1,269,219 square miles (3,287,263 square kilometers). Capital: New Delhi.

Indiana A midwestern state. Indiana became the nineteenth state in the United States in 1816. It has coal deposits, but manufacturing dominates the economy. Metals and transport equipment are major products. Grain, soybeans, fruits, and mint are grown. Area: 36,291 square miles (93,993 square kilometers). Capital: Indianapolis.

Indianapolis State capital of Indiana. It is famous

Built by the Mogul emperor Shah Jahan as a monument to his wife, the Taj Mahal is in the town of Agra in India.

for its annual auto race, the Indianapolis 500.

Indian Ocean Third-largest ocean in the world. Area: 28,350,000 square miles (76,000,000 square kilometers).

Indonesia Country in Asia. It is made up of many mountainous islands, including Java and Sumatra. Oil provides the most valuable industry. Crops include spices, coffee, and tea. Area: 741,101 square miles (1,919,443 square kilometers). Capital: Jakarta.

Indus River in Asia. Length: 1,800 miles (2,897 kilometers).

Innsbruck City in Austria.

Inverness Port and city in Scotland.

Ionian Islands Group of Greek islands in the Mediterranean Sea.

Ionian Sea Part of the Mediterranean Sea between Greece and Italy.

Iowa A midwestern state.

The beautiful green scenery of Kerry, a county in southwestern Ireland.

Iowa became part of the United States in 1803. In 1846 it became the twenty-ninth state. As a big farming state, Iowa's chief crops are soybeans and grain. Cattle and pigs are raised. Manufacturing and food processing are important. Area: 56,290 square miles (145,790 square kilometers). Capital: Des Moines.

Iran Islamic country in Asia. Its economy is based on oil. Agriculture includes some goat and sheep farming. Area: 636,372 square miles (1,648,000 square kilometers). Capital: Tehran.

Iraq Country in Asia. Its economy is based on the large oil fields of the north. There is some agriculture in the fertile areas. Area: 169,235 square miles (438,317 square kilometers). Capital: Baghdad.

Ireland Island in the Atlantic Ocean. It is divided into Northern Ireland (part of the United Kingdom) and the Republic of Ireland.

Ireland, Republic of Independent country in Europe. It occupies most of the island of Ireland. It has a mild, damp climate with an agricultural economy. Tourism and manufacturing are also important. Area: 27,137 square miles (70,000 square kilometers). Capital: Dublin.

Irish Sea Part of the Atlantic Ocean bounded by Ireland, England, Scotland, and Wales.

Irrawaddy River in Burma. Length: 1,250 miles (2,000 kilometers).

Islamabad Capital city of Pakistan.

Israel Country in southwest Asia on the Mediterranean coast. The landscape ranges from desert to fertile coastal plains. Leading exports are citrus fruits and vegetables. Industries range from textiles to electronic equipment. Tourism is also important. Area: 7,992 square miles (20,770 square kilometers). Capital: Jerusalem.

A tropical climate and fertile soil make Indonesia's islands a paradise for plants.

The maharajah's City Palace in Jaipur, India.

Istanbul Port and city in Turkey.

Italy Country in Europe. It consists of a mainland and two islands, Sicily and Sardinia. The Po Valley in the north is the main agricultural region. Millions of tourists enjoy Italy's Mediterranean climate and cultural history. Area: 116,324 square miles (301,000 square kilometers). Capital: Rome.

Ivory Coast Country in Africa. It has tropical rain forests as well as large treeless plains. Most of the people are farmers who raise only enough food for themselves. Coffee and cocoa are the main cash crops and exports. Area: 124,504 square miles (322,463 square kilometers). Capital: Abidjan.

J

Jackson State capital of Mississippi. It became the capital in 1821. The city was largely destroyed in 1863, during the Civil War.

Jacksonville Port and city in Florida.

Jaipur City in India.

Jakarta Capital city of Indonesia.

Jamaica Mountainous island country in the Caribbean Sea. It has a warm, moist climate. Sugar cane, bananas, coffee, fruit, coconuts, and ginger are grown. Tourism is important. Area: 4,244 square miles (10,964 square kilometers). Capital: Kingston.

Japan Country in eastern Asia. It is made up of four large islands and three thousand smaller ones. Fishing is important. Farms produce rice, barley, wheat, and tea. Japan is one of the largest industrial nations in the world. It exports ships, cars, motorcycles, and electronic goods. Area: 145,870 square miles (377,708 square kilometers). Capital: Tokyo.

Japan, Sea of Part of the Pacific Ocean, between Japan, Korea, and the U.S.S.R.

Java Island of Indonesia. It contains the nation's capital, Jakarta.

Jefferson City State capital of Missouri. It is a trade center.

Jerusalem Capital city of Israel.

Jiddah Port and city in Saudi Arabia.

Johannesburg City in South Africa.

Jordan Country in the Middle East. It borders Syria, Iraq, Saudi Arabia, and Israel. Jordan has large areas of desert with little vegetation. Some crops are grown in irrigated valleys. Area: 37,738 square miles (97,740 square kilometers). Capital: Amman.

Juneau State capital of Alaska. It was settled after gold was discovered in 1880. The city is now an important fishing center.

Jutland Peninsula of northern Europe. It consists of mainland Denmark and northwest Germany.

K

K2 Second-highest mountain in the world, on the border between China and Pakistan. It is also called Mount Godwin Austen. Height: 28,250 feet (8,611 meters).

Kabul Capital city of Afghanistan.

Kalahari Large desert region in southern Africa. Area: 200,000 square miles (520,000 square kilometers).

Kampala Capital city of Uganda.

Kampuchea (formerly called Cambodia) Country in Southeast Asia. Most of the people live in the central plains of the country, where they grow rice. The rest of the land is forested. Area: 69,898 square miles (181,000 square kilometers). Capital: Phnom Penh.

Kanchenjunga, Mount Mountain in the Himalayas. It is the third-highest mountain in the world. Height: 28,208 feet (8,598 meters).

Kansas A midwestern state. Kansas lies midway between the Atlantic and Pacific oceans. It became a United States territory in 1803 and the thirty-fourth state in 1861. Kansas is a major beef and wheat producer. It also produces oil and natural gas, transport equipment, machinery, and food products. Area: 82,264 square miles (213,063 square kilometers). Capital: Topeka.

Kansas City Name of two midwestern cities in the United States. The cities are on the state line between Kansas and Missouri. Both are important commercial and agricultural centers.

Karachi Port and city in Pakistan.

Kara Sea Part of the Arctic Ocean. It is frozen for most of the year.

Katmandu Capital city of Nepal.

Kazan Port and city in the U.S.S.R.

Kentucky State in the east-central region of the United States. Kentucky became the fifteenth state in 1792. Kentucky is known for its bluegrass, on which racehorses graze, and for its tobacco. Farmland covers more than half of the state, and soybeans, grain, and wheat are grown. Beef cattle, milk, pork, eggs, and poultry are leading products. The state leads all others in coal production. Manufacturing of transport equipment and machinery is a chief activity. Area: 40,395 square miles (104,659 square kilometers). Capital: Frankfort.

Kenya's game reserves. Here elephants and other wild animals are protected.

Kenya Country in Africa. Kenya's forests yield timber products. The chief exports are coffee, tea, sugar, cereals, and grain. Tourists visit the game preserves. Area: 224,961 square miles (582,800 square kilometers). Capital: Nairobi.

Clay pots lined up for sale in the city of Katmandu.

Kenya, Mount Volcanic mountain in Kenya. Height: 17,058 feet (5,200 meters).

Khartoum Capital city of Sudan.

Kiev City in the U.S.S.R.

Kigali Capital city of Rwanda.

Kilimanjaro Volcanic mountain in Tanzania. Height: 19,340 feet (5,899 meters).

Kingston Capital city of Jamaica.

Kinshasa Port and capital city of Zaire.

Kiribati Country in the Pacific Ocean. It consists of a string of islands with poor soil but a good climate. The chief crop is coconuts, and the main food is fish. Area: 281 square miles (728 square kilometers). Capital: Tarawa.

Kishinev City in the U.S.S.R.

Kitchener City in Ontario, Canada.

Kobe Port and city in Japan.

Kodiak Island Mountainous island off the coast of Alaska. It is an important fishing center, particularly for salmon. It is also the home of the Kodiak bear, largest of all bears.

Korea East Asian peninsula between the Sea of Japan and the Yellow Sea. Formerly one country, it was divided into two countries in 1948. The two countries are the Democratic People's Republic of Korea and the Republic of Korea.

Korea, Democratic People's Republic of (usually called North Korea) Country occupying the northern part of the Korean Peninsula. It has a cold climate. People work on collective farms and in state-owned factories. Minerals include coal, iron ore, and tungsten. Area: 46,540 square miles (120,538 square kilometers). Capital: Pyongyang.

Korea, Republic of (usually called South Korea) Country occupying the southern region of the Korean Peninsula. The country is mountainous and hot. Rice is the main crop. Manufacturing is important. Partly because of foreign trade, South Korea is now a leading industrial power. Area: 38,025 square miles (98,484 square kilometers). Capital: Seoul.

Krakow Port and city in Poland.

Kuala Lumpur Capital city of Malaysia.

Kunming City in China.

Kuwait Country in the Middle East. It has become rich because of its great oil reserves. Most people were once herders, keeping sheep, goats, and camels. Today, Kuwait has free schools, hospitals, and other modern services thanks to its oil wealth. Area: 6,880 square miles (17,824 square kilometers). Capital: Kuwait.

Kuwait Port and capital city of Kuwait.

Kyoto City in Japan.

L

Labrador Peninsula in Canada. It contains large iron ore deposits.

Lagos Port and capital city of Nigeria.

Lahore City in Pakistan.

Lansing State capital of Michigan. It produces cars, trucks, and machinery.

Lanzhou City in China.

Laos Mountainous country in Asia. It is mostly covered with forests. Timber products, rice, coffee, and corn are important. Tin is the chief export. Area: 91,400 square miles (236,862 square kilometers). Capital: Vientiane.

La Paz Administrative capital city of Bolivia.

Las Palmas Port city in the Canary Islands.

Las Vegas City in Nevada. It is a major resort and tourist center.

Lausanne City in Switzerland.

Downtown Las Vegas, famous for its casinos and nightclubs.

Classical ruins in Lebanon, once an outpost of the Roman Empire.

Lebanon Country on the Mediterranean Sea. It has a warm climate and good rainfall. Cereals, fruits, and vegetables are grown in fertile areas. Lebanon has few minerals or industries. Area: 3,950 square miles (10,400 square kilometers). Capital: Beirut.

Le Havre Port and city in France.

Leipzig City in eastern Germany.

Le Mans City in France. It is famous for its yearly sports car race.

Leningrad Port and city in the U.S.S.R.

Lesotho Country in Africa. It has warm summers and cool winters. Wheat, barley, beans, and corn are grown in fertile areas. Area: 11,720 square miles (30,362 square kilometers). Capital: Maseru.

Liberia Country on the coast of west Africa. The climate is hot and wet. Rubber, iron, gold, and diamonds are exported. Liberia was founded in 1822 as a settlement for freed slaves from the United States. Area: 43,000 square miles (111,398 square kilometers). Capital: Monrovia.

Libreville Port and capital city of Gabon.

Libya Country in Africa. Most people live near the Mediterranean coast, raising livestock and growing crops. Libya's wealth comes from oil. Area: 679,362 square miles (1,759,540 square kilometers). Capital: Tripoli.

Liechtenstein Small European country. The land is mostly mountainous. Its economy relies heavily on tourism and finance. Area: 62 square miles (158 square kilometers). Capital: Vaduz.

Liege Port and city in Belgium.

Ligurian Sea Part of the Mediterranean Sea, north of Corsica.

Lille City in France.

Lilongwe Capital city of Malawi, in the south-central part.

Lima Capital city of Peru.

Limpopo River in South Africa. Length: 1,000 miles (1,600 kilometers).

Lincoln State capital of Nebraska. It is named after U.S. President Abraham Lincoln. Capital since 1867, the city is a trade center.

Lisbon Port and capital city of Portugal.

A downtown scene in Lisbon.

Lithuania Land on the eastern shore of the Baltic Sea.

Little Rock State capital of Arkansas. Founded in 1820, the city has an economy based on food processing and timber.

Liverpool Port and city in England.

Lodz City in Poland.

Logan, Mount Mountain in the Yukon Territory, Canada. It is the highest peak in the country and the second highest in North America. Height: 19,524 feet (5,951 meters).

Loire River in France. Length: 625 miles (1,006 kilometers).

Lome Port and capital city of Togo.

London Capital city of the United Kingdom. It is located in the southern part of England. Millions of tourists visit its historic buildings, such as the Tower of London, Westminster Abbey, and Buckingham Palace.

London City in Ontario, Canada.

Londonderry (also known as Derry) Port and city in Northern Ireland.

Los Angeles Port and city in southern California. It is a major industrial center.

Louisiana A state in the southern United States. It was once part of the enormous French colony of Louisiana, which the United States purchased in 1803. It became the eighteenth state in 1812. The climate is subtropical. Soybeans, sugar cane, and rice are major crops. Cattle are raised and many fish are caught. The leading mineral products are oil and natural gas. Chief manufactured goods are chemicals and food products. The largest city is New Orleans, a major international port. Area: 47,752 square miles (123,677 square kilometers). Capital: Baton Rouge.

Louisville Port and city in Kentucky. It is a major tobacco market and manufacturing center.

Luanda Capital city of Angola.

Harvesting grapes in a valley near the Loire.

The lake front at Lucerne.

Lucerne (Also spelled Luzern) City in Switzerland.

Lusaka Capital city of Zambia.

Luxembourg Small country in Europe. The north is forested and hilly. The south has a mild climate with rolling plains and good farmland. Luxembourg's wealth comes from industry, particularly iron and steel. Area: 999 square miles (2,585 square kilometers). Capital: Luxembourg.

Luxembourg Capital city of Luxembourg.

Luzon Largest island in the Philippines.

Lyons Port and city in France.

M

Macao (also spelled Macau) Portuguese territory along the southeast coast of China. Area: 6 square miles (15 square kilometers).

Mackenzie Longest river in Canada. Length: 1,071 miles (1,724 kilometers).

Madagascar Island country in the Indian Ocean. The chief crops are rice, coffee, vanilla, cloves, and bananas. Most people live by farming. Area: 226,658 square miles (587,194 square kilometers). Capital: Antananarivo.

Madison State capital of Wisconsin. It is an important trade and manufacturing center.

Madras Port and city in India.

Madrid Capital city of Spain.

Maine Largest of the New England states in the United States. Maine was part of Massachusetts from the late 1600s until 1820, when it became the twenty-third state. Maine has cool winters and short, warm summers. The scenic Acadia National Park attracts many tourists. Timber and paper industries, with tourism, form the basis of the economy. The main fishing port and largest city is Portland. Area: 33,215 square miles (86,026 square kilometers). Capital: Augusta.

Majorca Spanish island in the Mediterranean Sea.

Malabo Capital city of Equatorial Guinea.

Malawi Country in southeast Africa. Much of the land is made up of high, cool plateaus. Most people are farmers growing their own food. Some people work on plantations where crops such as tea and sugar are grown for export. Area: 45,747 square miles (118,515 square kilometers). Capital: Lilongwe.

Malaysia Country in Asia. It is made up of 13 states. Most states are on the mainland, West Malaysia. Two are in

East Malaysia on the island of Borneo. The country has a tropical climate. Most people live in West Malaysia. Much of East Malaysia is still wild. Crops include rice, pepper, and pineapples. Malaysia is the world's largest producer of rubber and tin. Area: 127,581 square miles (329,834 square kilometers). Capital: Kuala Lumpur.

Mali Country in west Africa. The northern part is in the Sahara Desert. Timbuktu, a town in central Mali, is the last town before travelers enter the northern desert. Southern Mali is farmed. Cotton, peanuts, and grains are grown. The people are mostly farmers and wandering herders. Area: 478,841 square miles (1,240,000 square kilometers). Capital: Bamako.

Malta Country in the Mediterranean Sea made up of several islands. Malta, the largest island, is high and rocky, with a flat central plain. People work in dockyards and tourist hotels. Area: 122 square miles (316 square kilometers). Capital: Valletta.

Man, Isle of Self-governing British island in the Irish Sea.

Managua Capital city of Nicaragua.

Manama Capital city of Bahrain.

Manchester City in England.

Manila Capital and largest city in the Philippines. It is a leading port and center of culture and commerce.

Manitoba A central Canadian province. It became Canada's fifth province in 1870. Nickel, copper, oil, and zinc are mined. Beef, dairy products, and wheat are the chief farm products. Manitoba has about 100,000 lakes. Area: 251,000 square miles (649,950 square kilometers). Capital: Winnipeg.

Maputo Port and capital city of Mozambique.

Mariana Islands Group of islands in the western

The Bunker Hill Monument in Charlestown, Boston, Massachusetts.

Pacific Ocean. The islands are part of the United States Trust Territory of the Pacific Islands.

Marmara, Sea of Sea between European and Asian Turkey.

Marshall Islands Group of islands in the western Pacific Ocean. They are part of the United States Trust Territory of the Pacific Islands.

Martinique Island in the Caribbean Sea. It belongs to France. Its main industry is sugar cane production. Area: 425 square miles (1,102 square kilometers). Capital: Fort-de-France.

Maryland One of the original 13 states in the United States. Maryland was the seventh to ratify the Constitution, in 1788. On the Atlantic coast is the port and city of Baltimore. Coal is mined, but manufacturing is the leading activity. Farmland covers almost half of Maryland. Poultry, milk, corn, soybeans, and tobacco are the chief farm products. Area: 10,460 square miles (27,092 square kilometers). Capital: Annapolis.

Maseru Capital city of Lesotho.

Massachusetts A New England state in the United States. It was the sixth state to ratify the Constitution, in 1788. Massachusetts is a manufacturing state. Dairy and farm products, as well as fishing, are also important. Area: 8,257 square miles (21,385 square kilometers). Capital: Boston.

Matterhorn Mountain in the Alps. It is on the border between Switzerland and Italy. Height: 14,691 feet (4,477 meters).

Mauritania Hot, dry country in Africa. In the south there is enough rainfall for farming. Fishing is also important. Iron ore is the country's chief resource. Area: 398,000 square miles (1,030,969 square kilometers). Capital: Nouakchott.

Mbabane Capital city of Swaziland.

McKinley, Mount Mountain in Alaska. It is located in Denali National Park and is the highest peak in North America. Height: 20,320 feet (6,198 meters).

Mecca Sacred city of the Moslem religion. It is located in Saudi Arabia.

Mediterranean Sea Large sea bounded by southern Europe, western Asia, and northern Africa.

Melbourne Port and city in Australia.

Memphis Port and city in Tennessee.

Mexico Country in Central America. It has mountains, volcanoes, and high plateaus. A wide, flat peninsula, the Yucatan, is in the southeast. The lowlands are hot and humid, the north dry, and the mountains much col-

The permanently snowy peak of the Matterhorn.

der. The forests provide timber. The farmland yields beans, coffee, cotton, fruit, and vegetables. Cattle and other livestock are raised. Minerals include gold, silver, and copper. Large oil reserves are helping to develop the nation's industry. Area: 758,136 square miles (1,963,564 square kilometers). Capital: Mexico City.

Mexico, Gulf of Part of the Atlantic Ocean. It is located on the southern coast of North America.

Mexico City Capital city of Mexico. It is the largest Latin American city and one of the largest cities in the world.

Miami Port and city in Florida. It is a major tourist resort.

Michigan A state in the midwestern United States. It is bordered by parts of four of the Great Lakes. The scenery attracts many visitors. Michigan became the twenty-sixth state to

join the Union, in 1837. It is a prosperous industrial state, known for its cars, machinery, and steel. There are farms in the south. The largest city is Detroit. Area: 58,527 square miles (151,586 square kilometers). Capital: Lansing.

Michigan, Lake Third-largest of the Great Lakes. It lies completely within the United States. Area: 22,300 square miles (57,757 square kilometers).

Middle East Large region that covers parts of southeastern Europe, northeastern Africa, and southwestern Asia. Some of the larger countries in the Middle East are Turkey, Iran, Iraq, Saudi Arabia, Egypt, and Sudan.

Milan City in Italy.

Milwaukee Port and city in Wisconsin. Set up as a fur trading post in 1795, it gradually expanded into a large industrial city.

Minneapolis Port and city in Minnesota. It is a major center for grain and computer electronics.

Minnesota A state in the midwestern United States. It was first populated by Indians and later by French fur traders. In 1858 it became the thirty-second state. It is a major food producing and iron-mining state. Manufactured goods include machinery, metal products, and food. Minnesota has thousands of lakes. Area: 84,402 square miles (218,601 square kilometers). Capital: Saint Paul.

Mississippi A state in the southern United States. It became the twentieth U.S. state in 1817. It has a warm, moist climate. Farming once dominated the economy, but now manufacturing is the leading activity. Manufactured goods include transport and electric equipment, timber, and food products. Mississippi produces some oil and natural gas. Area: 47,716 square miles (123,584 square kilometers). Capital: Jackson.

Mississippi Major river in the United States. It flows from northwestern Minnesota to the Gulf of Mexico. Length: 2,348 miles (3,779 kilometers).

Missouri A state in the midwestern United States. It became the twenty-fourth state in

Mississippi steamboat, *Delta Queen*, built in 1926 and still in service.

the United States in 1821. It is a major farming and industrial site. Lead and zinc are mined. Transport equipment, chemicals, and food products are manufactured. Soybeans, wheat, and corn are leading crops, and livestock is raised. The largest cities are Saint Louis and Kansas City. Area: 69,686 square miles (180,486 square kilometers). Capital: Jefferson City.

Missouri Major river in the United States. It is the main tributary of the Mississippi River, flowing through Missouri, Nebraska, Iowa, North and South Dakota, and Montana. It is used for irrigation. Length: 2,315 miles (3,726 kilometers).

Monaco One of the world's smallest countries. It is located on the southeast coast of France. Its Mediterranean climate, hotels, and government-owned casino attract many tourists. Area: 0.7 square mile (1.9 square kilometers). Capital: Monaco.

Mongolia Large country in east central Asia. It contains a high, windy plateau, mountains in the west, and the Gobi Desert in the south. The chief products are animal hides, wool, and livestock. Coal and oil reserves are being developed. Area: 604,000 square miles (1,565,406 square kilometers). Capital: Ulan Bator

Monrovia Port and capital city of Liberia. It was named after U.S. President James Monroe.

Montana A Rocky Mountain state. It is the fourth-largest state in the United States. Montana became the forty-first state in 1889. Vast areas of grazing land are found in the east. The Rocky Mountains are in the west. The leading farming activity is raising livestock. Wheat is the chief crop. Oil, coal, and copper are mined. Manufacturing includes timber and food products. Area: 147,138 square miles (381,086 square kilometers). Capital: Helena.

Monte Carlo Popular tourist resort in Monaco. It is famous for its gambling casino.

Montevideo Port and capital city of Uruguay.

Montgomery State capital of Alabama. The capital since 1846, it was the site of the formation of the Confederate States in 1861.

Montpelier State capital of Vermont. Montpelier dates from 1780 and has been the capital since 1805.

Montreal Port and city in Quebec, Canada. It is the second-largest French-speaking city in the world.

Morocco Country in northwest Africa. The people grow grains, fruits, olives, and vegetables. Tourism is also important. Area: 177,117 square miles (458,730 square kilometers). Capital: Rabat.

Moscow Capital city of the U.S.S.R. The Kremlin, Red Square, and Saint Basil's Church are among its famous landmarks.

Mozambique Country in Africa. It has a hot, rainy season and a cool, dry season. Farming is important. The chief product is cashew nuts. Coconuts, sugar cane, and cotton are also grown. Area: 308,642 square miles (799,380 square kilometers). Capital: Maputo.

Munich City in southern Germany.

Murmansk Port and city in the northwest of the U.S.S.R.

Murray River in Australia. Length: 1,596 miles (2,600 kilometers).

Muscat Port and capital of Oman.

N

Nagasaki Port and city in Japan.

Nairobi Capital city of Kenya.

Namibia Large, thinly populated territory in southwest Africa. It is mostly made up of deserts. Its economy depends heavily on diamonds. Area: 317,818 square miles (823,145 square kilometers). Capital: Windhoek.

Nanjing Port and city in China.

Naples Port and city in Italy.

Nashville State capital of Tennessee. It is important for trade and shipping and is a famous center for music.

Nassau Capital city of the Bahamas.

Nauru Tiny island nation in the central Pacific Ocean. It has no formal capital city. Area: 8 square miles (21 square kilometers).

Ndjamena Capital city of Chad.

Nebraska A state in the midwestern United States. Nebraska became the thirty-seventh state in 1867. Much of the land is open, treeless plains with very fertile soil. Nebraska is a major agricultural state. Beef and dairy cattle are raised on huge ranches. Corn, soybeans, and wheat are the chief crops. Manufacturing is also important. Area: 77,355 square miles (200,350 square kilometers). Capital: Lincoln.

Nepal Mountainous country in Asia. It is the site of Mount Everest. The people cultivate terraced fields on the mountain slopes. Nepal exports rice, timber, cereals, and cattle. Tourism is growing in importance. Area: 56,827 square miles (147,181 square kilometers). Capital: Katmandu.

A view across the city and bay of Naples to Mount Vesuvius.

Netherlands, The Small, low-lying country in Europe. It is also known as Holland. Canals and rivers crisscross the country. Windmills and fields of tulips are familiar sights. Farm products include grains, butter, cheese, flowers, and vegetables. Industries flourish despite the lack of minerals. The Netherlands has shipyards, manufacturing plants, and chemical works. It obtains energy from natural gas. Area: 14,405 square miles (37,310 square kilometers). Capital: Amsterdam.

Netherlands Antilles Group of Caribbean islands that is part of the Netherlands. Area: 308 square miles (798 square kilometers). Capital: Willemstad.

Nevada A Rocky Mountain state in the United States. It became the thirty-sixth state in 1864. It is thinly populated, but the scenery attracts many tourists. The discovery of silver in 1859 raised the area's population. Manufacturing and tourism are important. Dams, such as the famous Hoover Dam, generate hydroelectric power. Livestock is raised. Nevada's irrigated land produces wheat, fodder, and beef cattle. Area: 110,540 square miles (286,297 square kilometers). Capital: Carson City.

Newark Northeastern city in the state of New Jersey.

New Brunswick Province in eastern Canada. During and after the American Revolution, many Americans loyal to Britain settled in New Brunswick. In 1867 it became one of the four original provinces of Canada. Today, manufacturing, fishing, and farming are important. The province has zinc, lead, coal, and potash. Area: 28,354 square miles (73,440 square kilometers). Capital: Fredericton.

New Caledonia Group of mountainous islands in the Pacific Ocean. It is a territory of France. Capital: Noumea.

New Delhi Capital city of India. The former capital, Delhi, is only three miles (almost five kilometers) away.

New England Region in the northeastern United States. It contains Connecticut, Maine, Massachusetts, New Hampshire, Rhode Island, and Vermont.

Newfoundland Province in eastern Canada. Fishing, forestry, oil, and mining are important. Area: 156,649 square miles (405,720 square kilometers). Capital: Saint John's.

New Hampshire A New England state in the United States. It became the ninth state in 1788. Dairy and poultry farming are important, but manufacturing dominates the economy.

An oil platform in Conception Bay near Saint John's, Newfoundland.

Machinery, computers, and wood and paper products are made here. Tourism is important, as people come to the beaches in summer or the mountains in winter. Area: 9,304 square miles (24,097 square kilometers). Capital: Concord.

New Jersey A Mid-Atlantic state in the United States. New Jersey became the third state in 1787. Small but densely populated, New Jersey is a major manufacturing center. Chemicals, food products, and machinery are made here. Vegetables and dairy products are also common. New Jersey has a fine climate and many tourist resorts. Newark and Jersey City are the largest urban areas. Area: 7,836 square miles (20,295 square kilometers). Capital: Trenton.

New Mexico State in the southwest United States. It is the fifth-largest state. It became the forty-seventh state in 1912. The Rocky Mountains, Carlsbad Caverns National Park, and Spanish missions, frontier forts, and the ruins of pueblos attract many tourists. The chief resources are oil and natural gas, uranium, potash, copper, and coal. Cattle and sheep ranching are important. Irrigated farms produce cotton, hay, and wheat. Area: 121,666 square miles (315,113 square kilometers). Capital: Santa Fe.

New Orleans Port and city in Louisiana. It is a trade center for food and oil products. Tourism is also an important industry.

New South Wales State in southeast Australia. Area: 309,433 square miles (801,600 square kilometers). Capital: Sydney.

New York A Mid-Atlantic state in the United States. New York became the eleventh state in 1788. In the east is the

Rue Conti meets Rue Royal in the French Quarter, New Orleans.

scenic Appalachian Plateau. In the west are lakes Ontario and Erie. These lakes are linked by the Niagara River, which flows over Niagara Falls. Manufacturing is the leading source of income. Products include printed materials, instruments, machinery, and equipment. In addition to New York City, Buffalo and Rochester are major industrial centers. Farming is also important, with fruits, vegetables, and meat as major products. Area: 49,108 square miles (127,189 square kilometers). Capital: Albany.

New York City Principal American port and largest city in the United States. It is located on the Atlantic coast of New York State. It is divided into five boroughs: Manhattan, the Bronx, Queens, Brooklyn, and Staten Island. It was founded in 1625 as New Amsterdam by the Dutch West India Company. The company bought Manhattan from the Indians for about twenty-four dollars' worth of trinkets. The World Trade Center, Empire State Building, Statue of Liberty, and the United Nations Building are world-famous sites. Tourists are also attracted by New York City's parks, galleries, and theaters.

New Zealand Country in the southwest Pacific Ocean. It is made up of two main islands, North Island and South island, and several smaller islands. The climate is temperate with good rainfall. Most New Zealanders live in cities, but farming is an important activity. Industries include manufacturing and the production of timber and paper. Area: 103,883 square miles (269,057 square kilometers). Capital: Wellington.

Niagara Falls Two large waterfalls in North America. They are located on the Niagara River on the border between Canada and the United States. The falls are named Horseshoe Falls and the American Falls. They provide hydroelectric power and are a major tourist site. Height: Horseshoe Falls, 167 feet (51 meters); American Falls, 176 feet (54 meters).

Niamey Capital city of Niger.

Nicaragua Country in Central America. It has both Atlantic and Pacific Ocean coastlines, as well as several active volcanoes. The climate is hot and tropical. Earthquakes are common. Most people are farmers producing cotton, corn, beef, rice, bananas, and timber. Gold is mined. Area: 50,200 square miles (130,000 square kilometers). Capital: Managua.

Nice Port and city in France.

Nicosia Capital city of Cyprus.

Niger Country in Africa. It borders on the Sahara Desert and is a hot, dry land. Farming is possible near the Niger River. Many people live by herding animals. Uranium is an important export. Other minerals include tin and iron. Area: 489,200 square miles (1,267,000 square kilometers). Capital: Niamey.

Niger River in Africa. Length: 2,600 miles (4,180 kilometers).

Nigeria Country in Africa. The north is hot and dry, but farther south the climate is wetter. The coasts are fringed with mangrove swamps. People live by farming, forestry, and fishing. Oil and natural gas provide most of the national income. There are some minerals, and manufacturing is important. Area: 356,669 square miles (923,768 square kilometers). Capital: Lagos.

Feluccas, the flat-bottomed boats that have been used on the Nile since ancient times, cluster on the riverbank at Aswan.

Nile River in Africa. It is one of the longest rivers in the world. Length: 4,145 miles (6,680 kilometers).

Norfolk Port and city in Virginia. It is a major United States naval base and important shipbuilding center.

North America Third-largest continent. It contains Canada, the United States, Mexico, the countries in Central America, Greenland, and the islands in the West Indies. North America's highest mountain is Mount McKinley, which stands 20,320 feet (6,198 meters) high. Its longest river is the Mississippi, which is 2,348 miles (3,779 kilometers) long. Area: 9,360,000 square miles (24,241,000 square kilometers).

North Carolina A state in the southern United States. It became the twelfth state in 1789. Manufacturing is the chief source of income.

Selling glass beads in a Nigerian market.

Textiles and chemicals are leading products. Major farm products include soybeans, corn, peanuts, and tobacco, as well as poultry and eggs. The largest cities are Charlotte and Greensboro. Area: 52,669 square miles (136,413 square kilometers). Capital: Raleigh.

North Dakota A state in the midwestern United States. It became the thirty-ninth state in 1889. Farming is the leading economic activity. Wheat is the chief crop. Flax, sunflower seeds, and barley are also produced. Mining is important, and there are reserves of oil and coal. Food processing is a leading manufacturing industry. Area: 70,665 square miles (183,022 square kilometers). Capital: Bismarck.

Northern Ireland Part of the United Kingdom. Geographically, it is part of Ireland. The farmland is rich, and the climate is mild and moist. Industries include textiles and shipbuilding. Area: 5,462 square miles (14,000 square kilometers). Capital: Belfast.

Northern Territory Tropical state in Australia. Area: 519,800 square miles (1,346,200 square kilometers). Capital: Darwin.

North Pole Imaginary point near the center of the Arctic Ocean.

North Sea Part of the Atlantic Ocean. It is located between Great Britain and northern Europe. Area: 218,178 square miles (565,078 square kilometers).

Northwest Territories Vast region in northern Canada. It was acquired by Canada in 1870. Mining is the chief economic activity. Gold, oil, zinc, and other minerals are produced. Area: 1,322,910 square miles (3,426,320 square kilometers). Capital: Yellowknife.

Norway Country in northern Europe. It is covered mostly with rocks and forests. Farmers grow grains, potatoes, and vegetables. Fishing is important. The main industries are timber, petroleum, and mineral processing. Area: 149,405 square miles (386,958 square kilometers). Capital: Oslo.

Nouakchott Port and capital city of Mauritania.

Nova Scotia A province of eastern Canada. It was one of the four provinces that formed the original Dominion of Canada in 1867. Farms produce milk, fruits, and meat. Fishing is important as well as the manufacturing of food products, paper, and transportation equipment. Area: 21,425 square miles (55,490 square kilometers). Capital: Halifax.

Novaya Zemlya Group of islands in the Arctic Ocean that belong to the U.S.S.R.

Novgorod City and port in the U.S.S.R.

Nuremburg City in southern Germany.

Ellesmere Island, the largest island in Canada's Northwest Territories, is high in the Arctic and icebound for most of the year.

O

Oakland Port and city in California.

Ob River in the U.S.S.R. Length: 2,268 miles (3,650 kilometers).

Oder River in central Europe. Length: 530 miles (855 kilometers).

Odessa Port and city in western U.S.S.R.

Ohio A state in the midwestern United States. It became the seventeenth state in 1803. The Appalachian plateau makes up most of eastern Ohio. The west is a region of rolling plains. Soybeans and corn are leading crops. Livestock, including dairy and beef cattle, pigs, and poultry, is important. Coal, natural gas, and oil are mined. The main source of income is manufacturing. Leading manufactured goods are transport equipment, farm machinery, and metals. Area: 41,330 square miles (107,044 square kilometers). Capital: Columbus.

Oklahoma State located in the southwestern United States. Oklahoma became the forty-sixth state in 1907. It is a prosperous state, ranking among the highest in oil production. Manufacturing of machinery and metal products is the most important activity. Farming also makes a contribution to the economy,

A furnace for melting iron. Ontario is Canada's largest iron and steel manufacturer.

particularly cattle raising and wheat growing. Area: 69,919 square miles (181,089 square kilometers). Capital: Oklahoma City.

Oklahoma City State capital of Oklahoma. Grain marketing and food processing are major activities. The city began to expand rapidly after oil was struck in 1928.

Olympia State capital of Washington. It has been the capital since 1853.

Olympus, Mount Mountain in Greece. Height: 9,570 feet (2,911 meters).

Omaha Port and city in Nebraska. In the mid-1800s, it was a supply point for the westward migration. It is now a large meat-processing center.

Oman Country on the coast of the Arabian Peninsula. Although mainly desert, it has grown wealthy from its oil reserves. Area: 82,030 square miles

(212,441 square kilometers). Capital: Muscat.

Ontario Canadian province. It is one of the four provinces that made up the original Dominion of Canada in 1867. Manufactured goods include transport equipment, food products, and metal products. Gold, nickel, copper, silver, and uranium are mined. Beef cattle, fruits, pigs, and vegetables are leading farm products. Forestry is also important. Area: 412,582 square miles (1,068,580 square kilometers). Capital: Toronto.

Ontario, Lake Smallest of the Great Lakes. It has an area of 7,600 square miles (19,011 square kilometers). The United States-Canadian border passes through the center of the lake.

Oporto Port and city in Portugal.

Oran Port and city in Algeria.

Orange River River in South Africa. Length: 1,300 miles (2,100 kilometers).

Oregon State located on the Pacific coast of the United States. Oregon became the thirty-third state in 1859. It has a rugged coastline and mountains containing some volcanoes. Forests cover much of Oregon. Wood products are the leading manufactured goods, followed by food products. Hydroelectricity is produced at dams on the Columbia and several other rivers. Livestock products and wheat are important to the economy, as are salmon, sole, and other fish caught. Area: 96,981 square miles (251,180 square kilometers). Capital: Salem.

Orinoco River in Venezuela. Length: 1,284 miles (2,066 kilometers).

Orkney Islands Group of islands lying between the northern Atlantic Ocean and the North Sea. They belong to Great Britain.

Osaka Port and city in Japan.

Oslo Port and capital city of Norway.

Ottawa Capital city of Canada. It is located in the province of Ontario.

Ouagadougou Capital city of Burkina Faso.

Oxford City in England.

Ozarks, The Upland region of south-central United States. It extends from Arkansas to Oklahoma.

P

Pacific Islands All of the islands in the Pacific Ocean. They include such islands as Hawaii, New Zealand, the Marshall Islands, and Fiji.

Pacific Ocean Largest and deepest ocean in the world. It contains numerous volcanic islands. Area: 63,800,000 square miles (165,200,000 square kilometers).

Pakistan Country in southern Asia. Apart from the mountainous north and the river valley, it is mostly dry land. Crops of cereal, rice, cotton, and sugar cane are able to grow because of irrigation. Farmers also raise livestock. Industry is varied. Natural gas is an important resource. Area: 307,374 square miles (803,882 square kilometers). Capital: Islamabad.

View of the Willamette Valley, Oregon.

Palestine Land between Egypt and southwestern Asia on the Mediterranean Sea. Also known as the Holy Land, it was once divided between Israel and Jordan. Jordan gave up its claim in 1967, and Israel now occupies the entire area.

Panama Country lying on the narrow strip of land between North and South America. The Panama Canal runs across it. The climate is tropical. Rice is the main crop. Bananas, shrimps, sugar cane, and mahogany wood are exported. Area: 30,134 square miles (78,046 square kilometers). Capital: Panama City.

Panama Canal A ship canal 51 miles (82 kilometers) long cutting through the country of Panama. Completed in 1914, it connects the Caribbean Sea with the Pacific Ocean and provides a relatively short way between the Atlantic and the Pacific.

Panama City Port and capital city of Panama.

Papua New Guinea Country in the Pacific Ocean. Its climate is tropical. The central highlands are densely forested and are rich in minerals, especially copper. Coconuts, cocoa, coffee, rubber, palm oil, and tea are produced. Area: 178,704 square miles (462,840 square kilometers). Capital: Port Moresby.

Paraguay Country in central South America. Timber is a major product. The chief occupation is farming. Crops include cotton, rice, corn, soybeans, wheat, and tobacco. Area: 157,048 square miles (406,720 square kilometers). Capital: Asuncion.

Paramaribo Port and capital city of Suriname.

Paris Port and capital city of France. It is a major cultural, commercial, and fashion center. Famous buildings such as the Eiffel Tower and Cathedral of Notre Dame attract tourists.

An open-air exhibit in Montmartre, Paris. Seen behind the umbrella is the dome of Sacré Coeur, a cathedral.

Pearl Harbor American naval base on the island of Oahu in the Hawaiian Islands.

Pennsylvania A Mid-Atlantic state in the United States. Pennsylvania was first settled by people from Sweden and the Netherlands. In 1681 the Quaker William Penn founded a colony where Quakers and others could enjoy religious freedom. Pennsylvania became the second state in 1787. Coal is mined, and manufactured goods include metals, machinery, and food products. The largest city is Philadelphia. Area: 45,333 square miles (117,412 square kilometers). Capital: Harrisburg.

Persian Gulf Part of the Arabian Sea between the Arabian Peninsula and Iran.

Perth Capital city of Western Australia.

Peru Third-largest country in South America. It contains the Andes and part of the Amazon River. Many of the people are farmers growing cotton, coffee, and sugar cane. Most wealth comes from various minerals and oil. Area: 496,225 square miles (1,285,116 square kilometers). Capital: Lima.

Philadelphia Port and city in Pennsylvania. In the early 19th century it was the most important city in the United States and the nation's capital (1790-1800). The Declaration of Independence was signed there in 1776.

Philippines Country in southeast Asia. It is made up of over 7,000 islands. The climate is tropical, and there are frequent earthquakes. Crops include rice, corn, and coconuts. Copper and gold are important minerals.

The ruins of Machu Picchu, a fifteenth-century city in Peru.

Area: 115,800 square miles (299,976 square kilometers). Capital: Manila.

Phnom Penh Port and capital city of Kampuchea.

Phoenix State capital of Arizona. It is an electronics research center and popular winter resort.

Pierre State capital of South Dakota. The city is an agricultural trading center.

Pisa City in Italy.

Pittsburgh Port and industrial city in Pennsylvania. Its large iron and steel industry is based on its coal mines.

Plymouth Port in southwest England. The Pilgrims set sail for America from Plymouth in 1620.

Po River in Italy. Length: 405 miles (650 kilometers).

Poland Country in Europe. The land is mainly flat except for the hills and mountains in the south. This is the main area for farming, mining, and industry. Textiles, iron, steel, and machinery are major products. Minerals include lead, coal, zinc, and sulfur. Area: 120,727 square miles (312,654 square kilometers). Capital: Warsaw.

Popocatepetl Volcanic mountain in central Mexico. Height: 17,887 feet (5,452 meters).

Port-au-Prince Port and capital city of Haiti.

Portland Port and city of Oregon. It developed as a grain-exporting port and trade center in the 1800s.

Port Moresby Port and capital city of Papua New Guinea.

Port of Spain Port and capital of Trinidad and Tobago.

Porto-Novo Port and capital city of Benin.

Port Said Port and city of Egypt.

Portsmouth Port and city in southern England.

Prague, seen across the red roofs of the carefully preserved old quarter.

Portugal Country in western Europe. It relies heavily on manufacturing, farming, and fishing. Grains, fruits, olives, and figs are grown. Fine grapes and wine are produced. Portugal also produces cork, metals, and machinery. Area: 34,340 square miles (88,941 square kilometers). Capital: Lisbon.

Prague Capital city of Czechoslovakia.

Pretoria Administrative capital city of South Africa.

Prince Edward Island Smallest province of Canada. It joined the Dominion of Canada in 1873. Area: 2,184 square miles (5,660 square kilometers). Capital: Charlottetown.

Providence State capital of Rhode Island. It is a major port.

Puebla City in Mexico.

Puerto Rico Island in the Caribbean Sea, belonging to the United States. First discovered by Christopher Columbus in 1493, it has become a major sugar producer and a popular tourist center. Area: 3,515 square miles (9,103 square kilometers). Capital: San Juan.

Pyongyang Capital city of North Korea.

Pyrenees Mountain range in Europe. It forms a natural boundary between France and Spain.

A beach in the Algarve region of Portugal on the western edge of Europe.

Q

Qatar Small country in the Persian Gulf. Most people live in or around the capital, but some are still nomads. Qatar has grown rich from its oil reserves. Area: 4,400 square miles (11,000 square kilometers). Capital: Doha.

Quebec Canada's largest province. It is populated mainly by people of French ancestry, a number of whom speak only French. It became a Canadian province in 1867. Quebec is rich in natural resources, forestry, farming, and industry. The largest city and chief industrial center is Montreal. Area: 594,860 square miles (1,540,000 square kilometers). Capital: Quebec.

Quebec Port and capital city of the province of Quebec.

Queensland State in eastern Australia. Area: 667,000 square miles (1,727,200 square kilometers). Capital: Brisbane.

Quito Capital city of Ecuador.

R

Rabat Port and capital city of Morocco.

Raleigh State capital of North Carolina. It is a university and manufacturing center.

Rangoon Port and capital city of Burma.

A beautiful mosaic in the sixth-century Basilica of San Vitalis, Ravenna.

Ravenna Port city in northern Italy. It is famous for its mosaics. These are pictures made by fitting bits of stone, glass, or tile together.

Red River River in the United States. It flows from Texas to Louisiana. The name comes from the color of the water, which is caused by red clay. Length: 1,300 miles (2,090 kilometers).

Red Sea Sea between Africa and the Arabian Peninsula. It is connected with the Mediterranean Sea by the Suez Canal.

Regina Capital city of Saskatchewan, Canada.

Reims City in France.

Reykjavik Port and capital city of Iceland.

Rhine River in Europe. It flows from Switzerland through western Germany and the Netherlands into the North Sea. Length: 820 miles (1,320 kilometers).

Rhode Island Smallest state in the United States. In 1790 Rhode Island became the 13th state to ratify the Constitution. Located in southern New England, it has beautiful scenery and many historic buildings that attract tourists. Manufacturing dominates the economy. Jewelry, silverware, and metal products are the most valuable manufactured goods. The state has nurseries and dairy, poultry, and potato farms. Fishing is important on the coast. Area: 1,214 square miles (3,144 square kilometers). Capital: Providence.

Rhodes Greek island in the Aegean Sea.

Rhone River in southern France. Length: 507 miles (810 kilometers).

Richmond State capital of Virginia. Richmond has been the capital since 1780. It is a corporate and manufacturing center.

Riga Port and city in the U.S.S.R.

Rio de Janeiro Port and former capital city of Brazil.

Rio Grande River in North America. It flows from Colorado to the Gulf of Mexico. It forms part of the boundary between Mexico and the United States. Length: 1,885 miles (3,000 kilometers).

Riviera Narrow coastal land running between La Spezia in northwestern Italy and Hyeres in southern France along the Mediterranean Sea. It is famous for its beaches and sunny climate.

Riyadh Capital city of Saudi Arabia.

Rocky Mountains Mountain system in western North America. It runs from Alaska, along the western edge of Canada and the United States, to New Mexico.

Romania Mountainous country in Europe. The climate is warm in summer and very cold in winter. In the west and south are fertile plains. Corn, potatoes, grapes, and sugar beets are grown. The central mountains are forested and rich in minerals. Area: 91,699 square miles (237,482 square kilometers). Capital: Bucharest.

Rome Capital city of Italy. It is a major religious, cultural, and tourist center.

Rotorua City of central North Island, New Zealand.

Rotterdam Port and city in the Netherlands.

Rwanda Small, heavily populated country in Africa. The western part of the country is mountainous. The climate is warm. Most of the people are farmers growing bananas, sweet potatoes, and sorghum. Area: 10,169 square miles (26,336 square kilometers). Capital: Kigali.

S

Saarbrucken City in western Germany.

Sacramento State capital of California. It expanded greatly with the discovery of gold nearby in 1848. Now it is the site of three Air Force bases and various industries.

Sahara Largest desert in the world. It is located in northern Africa. Area: 3,500,000 square miles (9,000,000 square kilometers).

Saint Elias Mountains Mountain range in Alaska and western Canada.

Saint John Port and city in the province of New Brunswick, Canada.

Saint John's Port and capital city of Newfoundland, province in Canada.

Saint Kitts-Nevis Small nation in the Caribbean Sea. It is made up of two islands, St. Kitts (officially called St. Christopher) and Nevis. It

A geyser erupts in Rotorua, famous for its hot springs.

has a pleasant climate, and tourism is rapidly developing. Area: 103 square miles (260 square kilometers). Capital: Basseterre.

Saint Lawrence River in Canada. It flows northeastward from Lake Ontario into the Gulf of Saint Lawrence. The Saint Lawrence Seaway, a system of canals and locks on the river, opened the way for ocean-going vessels to reach the Great Lakes. The river also provides hydroelectric power to Canada and the United States. Length: 800 miles (1,287 kilometers).

Saint Lawrence, Gulf of Part of the North Atlantic Ocean. It is bordered by Nova Scotia, Newfoundland, and New Brunswick.

Saint Louis Port and city in Missouri. Located on the Mississippi River, it is an important manufacturing and transport center.

Saint Lucia Small island country in the West Indies. Its terrain is mountainous. Bananas and coconuts are among its main exports. Area: 240 square miles (620 square kilometers).

Saint Paul State capital of Minnesota. It has light industries and is a transportation center.

Saint Vincent and the Grenadines Island country in the Caribbean Sea. Area: 150 square miles (388 square kilometers). Capital: Kingstown.

Salem State capital of Oregon, in the northwestern part of the state.

Salt Lake City Capital city of Utah. Founded by Mormons in 1847, it is the center of the Mormon religion. It has varied industries, including electronics and oil refining.

Salzburg City in Austria.

Samarkand City in the U.S.S.R.

Samoa Islands Group of islands in the southwest Pacific Ocean. The islands are divided into Western Samoa, an independent nation, and American Samoa, which is part of the United States.

Sana Capital city of the Republic of Yemen.

San Diego Port and city in California. It has a naval base and large aerospace and shipbuilding industries. It also has a famous zoo and an ocean research center.

San Francisco Port and city in California. It is a major business center. The scenic waterfront and Golden Gate Bridge attract many tourists. Public transport in the city includes its famous cable cars. In 1906 and 1989 the city was damaged by earthquakes.

San Jose Capital city of Costa Rica.

San Jose City in California. It is in the center of a major fruit and vegetable growing area, and food processing and distribution are major activities.

San Juan Port and capital city of Puerto Rico.

The Capitol in Salt Lake City, Utah.

San Marino One of the smallest countries in the world. Located within Italy, it earns money largely from tourism and the sale of stamps. Area: 24 square miles (60 square kilometers). Capital: San Marino.

San Salvador Capital city of El Salvador in Central America.

Santa Fe State capital of New Mexico. It is the oldest capital city in the United States. Founded in 1609 by the Spanish, it is now an important tourist and administrative center.

Santiago Capital city of Chile.

Santo Domingo Port and capital city of the Dominican Republic.

Sao Paulo City in Brazil.

Sarajevo City in Yugoslavia.

Sardinia Self-governing island in the Mediterranean Sea, belonging to Italy.

Saskatchewan A central Canadian province. It is the leading wheat-growing province. Mining and manufacturing are also important. Area: 251,700 square miles (652,330 square kilometers). Capital: Regina.

Saskatoon City in Saskatchewan, Canada.

Saudi Arabia Country occupying most of the Arabian Peninsula. Wealth from oil discovered in 1933 has made Saudi Arabia an important nation in the Middle East. Area: 830,000 square miles (2,149,690 square kilometers). Capital: Riyadh.

Sault Sainte Marie Port and town in Ontario, Canada. It lies opposite the United States town of the same name, in Michigan.

Scandinavia Name given to the peninsula that contains Norway and Sweden. However, Denmark is also considered part of the Scandinavian region.

Scotland Part of the United Kingdom. Much of the country is mountainous, with islands and deep lakes in the west. Most Scots work in offices and factories. Area: 30,414 square miles (78,000 square kilometers). Capital: Edinburgh.

Seattle Largest city in Washington state. It is a commercial center, port, and industrial city. It has important aircraft, lumber, and other industries.

Seine River in France. Length: 475 miles (764 kilometers).

Senegal Country in Africa. It has plains in the center and tropical forests in the south. Its products include fish, peanut oil, and phosphates. Area: 75,750 square miles (196,192 square kilometers). Capital: Dakar.

Seoul Capital city of South Korea.

Severn River in England. Length: 220 miles (344 kilometers).

Seville Port and city in Spain.

Seychelles Country in the Indian Ocean. It is made up of about 90 islands. Tourism is the main industry. Area: 175 square miles (453 square kilometers). Capital: Victoria.

Shanghai Port and city in China.

Shannon Longest river in the Republic of Ireland. It is 240 miles (386 kilometers) long.

Shenyang City in China.

Shetland Islands Group of islands in the Atlantic Ocean, belonging to Great Britain.

Siberia Thinly populated region in northeastern Asia. It makes up about half of the U.S.S.R. It is rich in natural resources, including oil, diamonds, and gold. Area: 4,235,000 square miles (10,970,000 square kilometers).

Sicily Self-governing Italian island. Located in the Mediterranean Sea, it has a mountainous landscape.

Sierra Leone Hot, damp country in western Africa. Diamonds, palm oil, coffee, ginger, and cocoa are the main products. People grow rice, peanuts, and oranges for food. Area: 27,699 square miles (71,735 square kilometers). Capital: Freetown.

Sierra Nevada Mountain range in California. The highest peak is Mount Whitney. It is 14,494 feet (4,418 meters) high.

Singapore Island country in Asia. It has a tropical climate and is a busy, prosperous port and manufacturing center. Area: 240 square miles (580 square kilometers). Capital: Singapore.

Society Islands Group of islands in the Pacific Ocean, belonging to France.

Sofia Capital city of Bulgaria.

The old city of Shanghai houses the famous Yu-Yuan Garden, built during the sixteenth century.

Solomon Islands Island nation in the southern Pacific Ocean. Most people live by farming and fishing, and fish and timber are both exported. Area: 10,640 square miles (27,556 square kilometers). Capital: Honiara.

Somalia Hot, dry country in Africa. Herds of animals graze on most of the land. Drought and famine are serious problems. Area: 246,201 square miles (637,657 square kilometers). Capital: Mogadishu.

(1,221,037 square kilometers). Capitals: Pretoria (administrative), Cape Town (legislative), Bloemfontein (judicial).

South America Fourth-largest continent. It contains 12 independent countries. By far the largest of these is Brazil. The smallest is Suriname. South America's highest mountain is Mount Aconcagua, which stands 22,835 feet (6,965 meters) high. Its longest river is the Amazon, which is 4,000

miles (6,500 kilometers) long. Area: 6,887,000 square miles (17,837,000 square kilometers).

South Australia State in Australia. Area: 380,070 square miles (984,000 square kilometers). Capital: Adelaide.

South Carolina One of the southern states in the United States. South Carolina became the eighth state in 1788. The coastal plain contains swamps and forests. Inland, the land rises to the Blue Ridge, part of the Appalachian Moun-

The ancient walled "old city" of Sousse in Tunisia.

Sousse Port and city in Tunisia. It is a popular seaside resort.

South Africa Country at the southern tip of Africa. Wheat and fruit are exported. There are rich mineral resources, including gold, coal, copper, uranium, and diamonds. Area: 471,445 square miles

Kruger Park, the largest national park in South Africa, is home to zebras and many other wild animals.

tains. Textiles, chemicals, and machinery are manufactured. Soybeans, tobacco, and corn are major farm products. Area: 31,055 square miles (80,432 square kilometers). Capital: Columbia.

South China Sea Part of the Pacific Ocean. It is surrounded by Vietnam, the Philippines, Borneo, and south China.

South Dakota A state in the midwestern United States. It is mainly a flat region. The Black Hills in the southwest contain the Mount Rushmore National Memorial. South Dakota became the fortieth state in 1889. Farmland covers much of the state. Barley, beef cattle, pigs, oats, sheep, and wheat are major products. Gold is the chief mineral. The leading manufactured goods are food products and machinery. Area: 77,047 square miles (199,551 square kilometers). Capital: Pierre.

South Pole Imaginary point near the center of Antarctica.

Spain Country in Europe. It includes the Canary and Balearic islands. Much of Spain is a high, fairly dry plateau that is cold in winter and hot in summer. Tourism is an important industry. Wheat, barley, fruit, and vegetables are grown. Sheep and goats are raised. Wine is an important export. In-

Tossa de Mar in Spain, along the Mediterranean coast.

dustries include the manufacturing of automobiles, ships, and steel. Area: 194,898 square miles (504,742 square kilometers). Capital: Madrid.

Springfield State capital of Illinois. It is the burial place of U.S. President Abraham Lincoln.

Sri Lanka Island country off the southeast tip of India. It was formerly called Ceylon. The climate is hot with monsoon rains. Tropical forests cover large areas. Crops include tea, rubber, coconuts, and rice. Emeralds and rubies are mined. Area: 25,332 square miles (65,605 square kilometers). Capital: Colombo.

Stockholm Port and capital city of Sweden.

Strasbourg City in France.

Stuttgart City in southern Germany.

Sucre Constitutional capital of Bolivia.

Sudan Africa's largest country. It is mainly desert in the north and green and fertile in the south. The Nile River flows through Sudan. Cotton, peanuts, sugar cane, and millet (a type of grass) are grown. Area: 967,500 square miles (2,505,813 square kilometers). Capital: Khartoum.

Sudbury City in Ontario, Canada.

Suez Canal Major canal connecting the Mediterranean Sea with the Red Sea. The canal was opened in 1869. Length: 118 miles (190 kilometers).

Sumatra Large island of Indonesia. It is densely forested.

The Alps, high above the gentle Swiss countryside.

Superior, Lake Largest of the Great Lakes. It covers an area of 31,700 square miles (82,103 square kilometers). Its greatest depth is 1,330 feet (405 meters).

Suriname Country in South America. It has a tropical climate. Chief products are bauxite, sugar, fruit, rice, and timber. Area: 63,037 square miles (163,265 square kilometers). Capital: Paramaribo.

Swaziland Country in southern Africa. It is rich in mineral deposits and farmland. Its chief products are corn and sugar cane. Area: 6,700 square miles (17,360 square kilometers). Capital: Mbabane.

Sweden Country in Europe. It is part of Scandinavia. It has a cool climate with cold winters and mild summers. Sweden has an abundance of forests, minerals, and waterpower, which provides electricity. It has one of the highest standards of living in the world. Area: 173,732 square miles (450,000 square kilometers). Capital: Stockholm.

Switzerland Country in central Europe enclosed by mountains. Finance and tourism are important as well as the production of high-quality goods and dairy products. The people speak German, French, Italian, and Romansh. Area: 15,943 square miles (41,284 square kilometers). Capital: Bern.

Sydney Port and capital city of New South Wales, Australia.

Syria Country on the Mediterranean Sea. Much of Syria is dry, but some regions have fertile farmland. Grains, fruit, grapes, olives, tobacco, and cotton are grown. Textiles are important. Area: 71,498 square miles (185,165 square kilometers). Capital: Damascus.

T

Tahiti Largest island in the Society Islands.

Taipei Capital city of Taiwan.

Taiwan Island off mainland China. It was once called Formosa. People grow rice, tea, and sugar cane but live mainly by working in businesses and factories. Area: 13,900 square miles (36,000 square kilometers). Capital: Taipei.

Taiyuan City in China.

Tallahassee State capital of Florida. It is a government and university center.

Tampa City in Florida. It is a popular winter tourist resort, famous for its fishing.

Tangier Port and city in Morocco.

Tanzania Country in Africa. It has many lakes and Africa's highest mountain, Kilimanjaro. Chief crops include cashew nuts, cloves, tea, bananas, cotton, corn, and coffee. Area: 364,881 square

Tangier in Morocco.

A Texas Longhorn.

miles (945,013 square kilometers).Capital: Dar es Salaam.

Tasmania Island off of southeastern Australia. It has been the country's smallest state since 1901. Area: 26,200 square miles (67,800 square kilometers). Capital: Hobart.

Tasman Sea Part of the Pacific Ocean between New Zealand and Australia.

Tegucigalpa Capital city of Honduras.

Tehran Capital city of Iran.

Tennessee A state in the southern United States. It became the sixteenth state in 1796. Chemicals, food products, and machinery are its chief manufactured goods. Coal and zinc are among its mining products. Dairy products, meat, soybeans, tobacco, and corn are all important. The largest cities are Memphis and Nashville. Area: 42,114 square miles (109,152 square kilometers). Capital: Nashville.

Texas Second-largest state in the United States. In 1845 Texas became the twenty-eighth state. It has huge reserves of oil and natural gas. Manufacturing is a major activity. The most important products include chemicals, machinery, petroleum, and coal. Texas is also a major farming state. Beef cattle are the most valuable source of farming income. Area: 266,807 square miles (691,030 square kilometers). Capital: Austin.

Thailand Hilly, forested country in Asia. Chief crops include rice, corn, and rubber. Tin and tungsten are mined, and there is natural gas offshore. The forests yield valuable timber. Area: 198,500 square miles (514,000 square kilometers). Capital: Bangkok.

Thames River in England. Length: 210 miles (340 kilometers).

Thimbu Capital city of Bhutan.

Tianjin City in China.

Tibet Region in central Asia known as the "Roof of the World." Tibet is a self-governing territory of China. Much of the land is a high, windswept plateau surrounded by even higher mountain ranges. Most of the land cannot be farmed, but barley is grown in some areas. Milk, meat, and fur are provided by yaks, which are a kind of ox.

Tijuana City in Mexico, near the United States border.

Timbuktu Town in Mali.

The great Potola palace in Lhasa, Tibet, was the home of the Dalai Lama until the Chinese occupation of 1951.

Tirane Capital city of Albania.

Titicaca Highest major lake in the world. It is 12,500 feet (3,810 meters) above sea level, located in South America. Area: 3,200 square miles (8,300 square kilometers).

Togo Country in western Africa. The climate is tropical. Swamps, forests, or savanna grasslands cover most of the country. The people are mostly farmers, and cocoa and coffee are the chief export crops. Area: 21,925 square miles (56,785 square kilometers). Capital: Lome.

Tokyo Port and capital city of Japan.

Toledo Port on Lake Erie and industrial city in Ohio.

Modern-day Tokyo, one of the largest cities in the world.

Tonga Country in the Pacific Ocean. Tonga, made up of about 150 islands, belongs to the Pacific Islands. They are volcanic or coral in origin. The people grow bananas and coconuts. Area: 289 square miles (748 square kilometers). Capital: Nukualofa.

Topeka Capital of the state of Kansas.

Toronto Port and capital city of the province of Ontario. It is located on Lake Ontario.

Trenton Capital of the state of New Jersey. Founded in 1679, it is an important manufacturing center.

Trinidad and Tobago Country in the Caribbean Sea that is made up of two islands. The climate is tropical. Oil and asphalt are the chief products. Tourism is very important. Area: 1,978 square miles (5,128 square kilometers). Capital: Port of Spain.

Tripoli Port and capital city of Libya.

Tucson City in the state of Arizona. It is a popular winter resort.

Tulsa City in the state of Oklahoma. It is the center of a large oil-producing region.

Tunis Port and capital city of Tunisia.

Tunisia Country in Africa with a hot climate. There are salt lakes inland and oases where date palms grow. The coastal region is fertile, and crops and grazing animals are raised there. Phosphates and

Traditional dress in Tunisia often includes silver work.

petroleum are major exports. Area: 63,170 square miles (163,610 square kilometers). Capital: Tunis.

Turin City in Italy.

Turkey Country in Europe and Asia. The coastal region is temperate and good for farming. Inland, livestock is raised where it is cold, dry, and mountainous. Industries include mining, textiles, food processing, and carpet weaving. Area: 301,382 square miles (780,576 square kilometers). Capital: Ankara.

Turks and Caicos Islands Group of islands southeast of the Bahamas. They are a British dependency.

Tuvalu Island country in the Pacific Ocean. It consists of small islands. Coconuts are the main crop. Area: 10 square miles (26 square kilometers). Capital: Funafuti.

U

Uganda Country in Africa. A highland country, it is covered with forests, lakes, and mountains. Its people are mainly farmers. Coffee, tea, cotton, and other crops are grown. There are also factories and some mining. Area: 91,134 square miles (236,019 square kilometers). Capital: Kampala.

Ulan Bator Capital city of Mongolia.

Union of Soviet Socialist Republics (U.S.S.R.) Largest country in the world. It is spread over Europe and Asia. Because it is so huge, it is not really one country at all. It has over 90 different peoples, each with their own customs, beliefs, and histories. Of the 15 separate republics, the largest is the Russian Republic. Most of the industry is in the European part of the U.S.S.R. There are great mineral deposits and other natural riches in Siberia that are now being developed. Important crops in the U.S.S.R. are cereals, sugar beets, flax, hemp, and cotton. Industries include manufacturing, heavy engineering, and nuclear and aerospace technology. Area: 8,649,500 square miles (22,402,000 square kilometers). Capital: Moscow.

United Arab Emirates Country on the Persian Gulf. It is made up of seven small states. It is rich in oil, and it has prospered on the money earned from selling this oil. Area: 32,278 square miles (83,600 square kilometers). Capital: Abu Dhabi.

United Kingdom Short name for the United Kingdom of Great Britain and Northern Ireland. It is made up of England, Scotland, Wales, and Northern Ireland (see individual entries). Area: 94,250 square miles (245,050 square kilometers). Capital: London.

United States of America One of the richest and most powerful nations in the world. It stretches across North America

The United States Capitol.

from the Atlantic Ocean to the Pacific Ocean. It is made up of 50 states (see individual entries). The world's fourth-largest country, it has many different landscapes and climates. These range from the cold of Alaska to the tropical climate of Florida. Among the most spectacular sights are the Grand Canyon, Great Lakes, and Niagara Falls. Farming is highly developed and mechanized. Industrially, the United States produces half the world's factory goods. It has coal, oil, natural gas, and other minerals in abundance. Area: 3,618,770 square miles (9,372,571 square kilometers). Capital: Washington, D.C.

Ural Mountains Mountain range in the U.S.S.R.

Uruguay Country in South America. It contains flat, grassy plains that are ideal for raising cattle and sheep. Grains, fruit, and sugar are grown. Industries include textiles, chemicals, oil refining, and food processing. Area: 68,037 square miles (176,215 square kilometers). Capital: Montevideo.

Utah A west-central state in the United States. Utah was won from Mexico in 1848. It became the forty-fifth state in 1896. Utah has spectacular scenery and five national parks.

Copper, petroleum, coal, uranium, gold, and other metals are mined in the state. Metal products, machinery, and transport equipment are made here. Farming is also important. Utah's largest city, Salt Lake City, is the world headquarters of the Mormon Church. Area: 84,899 square miles (219,889 square kilometers). Capital: Salt Lake City.

Utrecht City lying on the Rhine River in the Netherlands.

V

Vaduz Capital city of Liechtenstein.

Valencia City in Spain.

Valetta Port and capital city of Malta.

Vancouver Port and city in the province of British Columbia, Canada.

Vancouver Port and oldest city in the state of Washington.

Vancouver Island Island off the coast of British Columbia, Canada.

Vanuatu Hilly, forested island country in the Pacific Ocean. It has a warm, damp climate. People live by farming and fishing. There are a few industries. Manganese and coconut meat are sold abroad. Area: 5,700 square miles (14,763 square kilometers). Capital: Port-Vila.

Vatican City World's smallest independent state. It is located in Rome, Italy. It is the center of the Roman Catholic Church and the residence of the Pope. Area: 109 acres (44 hectares). Capital: Vatican City.

Venezuela Country in South America. It is one of the world's leading oil producers. Minerals include iron ore, bauxite, and gold. These natural resources, along with tropical plantation crops, cattle ranching, and manufacturing industries, have made Venezuela the richest country on the South American continent. Area: 352,145 square miles (912,050 square kilometers). Capital: Caracas.

Venice Italian city lying on

The Bridge of Sighs in Venice, overlooking a canal.

about 120 islands in the Adriatic Sea.

Vermont A New England state in the United States. Vermont joined the Union as the fourteenth state in 1791. Its mountains attract skiers and other tourists. Manufactured goods include machinery, printed materials, and metal products. Burlington is the largest city and industrial center. Milk is the leading farm product. Meat, poultry, eggs, potatoes, and grains are also important, as is maple syrup. Area: 9,614 square miles (24,900 square kilometers). Capital: Montpelier.

Vesuvius Volcano in Italy. Height: 4,190 feet (1,277 meters).

Victoria State in Australia. Area: 87,900 square miles (227,600 square kilometers). Capital: Melbourne.

Victoria Capital city of British Columbia, Canada.

Victoria Falls Large waterfall on the Zambezi River in Africa. The falls border Zambia and Zimbabwe. Height: 343 feet (105 meters) at the center.

Vienna Capital city of Austria.

Vientiane Capital city of Laos.

Vietnam Country in southeastern Asia. It has seacoast, mountains, forests, and fertile river valleys. Rice, rubber, and tea are among its farm products. Fishing is also important to the economy. Area: 127,242 square miles (329,556 square kilometers). Capital: Hanoi.

Vilnius City in Lithuania.

Virginia A state in the southern United States. The first permanent English settlement in America was founded in Jamestown, Virginia, in 1607. Virginia became the tenth state in 1788. Tobacco is a major crop. Corn, soybeans, wheat, and livestock products are also important. Manufacturing dominates the economy. Coal is the most important mining product. Manufactured goods include chemicals, food products, transport equipment, and electrical equipment and machinery. The scenic Appalachian Mountains in the west and Virginia's historic sites attract many tourists. Area: 40,767 square miles (105,586 square kilometers). Capital: Richmond.

Virgin Islands Group of islands in the Caribbean Sea, split into two groups. One group belongs to the United States, purchased from Denmark in 1917. The other group belongs to Britain. The islands are a popular tourist resort.

Volga River in the U.S.S.R. and longest river in Europe. Length: 2,293 miles (3,700 kilometers).

Volgograd Port and city in the U.S.S.R.

W

Wales Part of the United Kingdom. It is a land of mountains and river valleys. Sheep are raised on the hillsides. Tourism is developing in Wales, where the scenery is beautiful. Area: 8,016 square miles (21,000 square kilometers). Capital: Cardiff.

Warsaw Capital city of Poland.

Washington A Pacific Coast state in the United States. Washington contains magnificent coastal and mountain scenery. It became the forty-second state in 1889. Resources include forests and coal. Manufacturing is the chief activity, providing transportation equipment, timber, and food products. Crops are also important. Beef cattle and chickens are raised.

The largest cities are Seattle, Spokane, and Tacoma. Area: 68,192 square miles (176,616 square kilometers). Capital: Olympia.

Washington, D.C. Capital city of the United States of America. It was named after U.S. President George Washington, who chose the location in 1791. The White House, where the U.S. President lives and works, is in this city.

Waterloo Town in Belgium.

Wellington Capital city of New Zealand.

Western Australia Largest state in Australia. Area: 975,100 square miles (2,525,500 square kilometers). Capital: Perth.

Western Sahara Area on the northwest coast of Africa. It is claimed by Morocco. Area: 102,700 square miles (266,000 square kilometers).

Western Samoa Country in the Pacific Ocean. It is part of the Pacific

A city square in Warsaw, Poland.

Islands. The people live on volcanic islands, which are mountainous and thick with forests. Cocoa and bananas are grown. Area: 1,093 square miles (2,841 square kilometers). Capital: Apia.

West Indies Chain of islands in the Atlantic Ocean. The islands stretch from Florida to Venezuela. Its three major island groups are the Bahamas, the Greater Antilles, and the Lesser Antilles. Among the islands are Cuba, Jamaica, Puerto Rico, and Hispaniola (Dominican Republic and Haiti).

West Virginia A state in the southern United States. It was part of Virginia until 1861. In 1863 it became the thirty-fifth state. It lies in the Appalachian Mountains and is mostly a rugged, scenic area. It is a major mining state, producing coal, oil, and natural gas. Farming is less im-

portant, but a variety of crops is grown. Area: 24,181 square miles (62,629 square kilometers). Capital: Charleston.

Whitehorse Capital city of Yukon Territory, Canada.

Wichita City in Kansas. It is a major oil refining, food processing, and aircraft industry center.

Wight, Isle of Island in the English Channel.

Windhoek Capital city of Namibia.

Winnipeg Capital city of the province of Manitoba, Canada. It is one of the world's major wheat markets.

Wisconsin State in the midwestern United States. Wisconsin became the thirtieth state in 1848. It is known especially for its dairy products. However, manufacturing is the most valuable activity. Machinery, food products, paper products, metals, and transportation equipment are all

made here. Milwaukee is the largest city and one of the country's top industrial centers. Area: 56,154 square miles (145,438 square kilometers). Capital: Madison.

Wyoming A Rocky Mountain state in the United States. Wyoming became the forty-fourth state in 1890. Its mineral products include petroleum, natural gas, and uranium. Beef cattle are another leading product. Manufacturing is also important to the economy. The Grand Teton and Yellowstone national parks are among the tourist attractions. Area: 97,914 square miles (253,596 square kilometers). Capital: Cheyenne.

X

Xi'an City in China.

Y

Yangtze River in China. Also called the Chang Jiang. Length: 3,915 miles (6,300 kilometers).

Yaounde Capital city of Cameroon.

Yellowknife Capital city of Northwest Territories, Canada.

Yellow Sea Part of the Pacific Ocean between China and Korea.

Fort Laramie, Wyoming.

These ruins in Zimbabwe probably date from the fifteenth century.

Yellow dirt gives the sea its color.

Yemen, Republic of Country in the Middle East, occupying the southern corner of the Arabian Peninsula. For many years, Yemen was divided into two separate nations: the Arab Republic of Yemen (North Yemen) and the People's Democratic Republic of Yemen (South Yemen). On May 22, 1990, the two nations unified, becoming the Republic of Yemen. In fertile areas of the country, crops of dates, wheat, millet, barley, coffee, cotton, fruits, and vegetables are grown. There is also some fishing and oil. Area: 203,887 square miles (530,106 square kilometers). Capital: Sana.

Yugoslavia Mountainous country in Europe. Many people are farmers growing cereals, tobacco, fruits, and olives. Industries include iron and steel, wood products, and other manufacturing. Area: 98,766 square miles (255,785 square kilometers). Capital: Belgrade.

Yukon Territory Vast, mountainous region in northwestern Canada. It attracted world attention during the Klondike Gold Rush in 1897. Minerals, mainly lead, zinc, silver, and gold,

Zurich is the commercial and banking center of Switzerland, located on the lake of the same name.

are the main source of income. Tourism is also important. Area: 186,661 square miles (483,450 square kilometers). Capital: Whitehorse.

Z

Zaire One of the largest countries in Africa. It was formerly called the Congo. Most people work the land, growing food and crops for export, such as palm oil, coffee, and rubber. The country has valuable minerals, notably copper. Area: 905,365 square miles (2,345,000 square kilometers). Capital: Kinshasa.

Zambezi River in Africa. Length: 1,700 miles (2,736 kilometers).

Zambia Country in Africa with a cool climate. The soil is poor. Most of the economy is based on mining, mainly copper. Area: 290,586 square miles (752,554 square kilometers). Capital: Lusaka.

Zimbabwe Country in southern Africa. Much of the country is high savanna grassland. Tobacco, cotton, tea, and grains are grown, and cattle is raised. Copper, nickel, chrome, and other minerals are mined. Industry is developing. Area: 150,873 square miles (390,550 square kilometers). Capital: Harare.

Zurich City in Switzerland.

United States of America

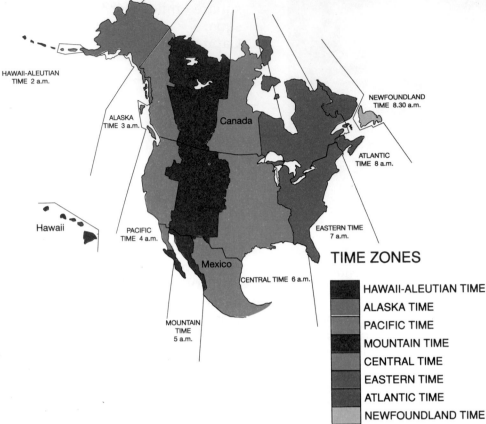

HAWAII-ALEUTIAN
TIME 2 a.m.

ALASKA
TIME 3 a.m.

Canada

NEWFOUNDLAND
TIME 8.30 a.m.

ATLANTIC
TIME 8 a.m.

Hawaii

PACIFIC
TIME 4 a.m.

EASTERN TIME
7 a.m.

Mexico

CENTRAL TIME 6 a.m.

MOUNTAIN
TIME
5 a.m.

TIME ZONES

HAWAII-ALEUTIAN TIME
ALASKA TIME
PACIFIC TIME
MOUNTAIN TIME
CENTRAL TIME
EASTERN TIME
ATLANTIC TIME
NEWFOUNDLAND TIME

The United States of America is a country of great variety. There are rich and dense subtropical forests. There is tundra – great stretches of frozen land where no trees will grow. There are plains and mountains, unspoiled wild places, and huge cities.

The people of the United States are as varied as the country they live in. Settlers who developed the country came from all over the world. They brought with them their own ways of life. These were in addition to the customs of the Native Americans, who were already there when the settlers arrived.

In area, the United States is the fourth-largest country in the world. Only the Union of Soviet Socialist Republics (U.S.S.R.), Canada, and China exceed its 3,618,770 square miles (9,372,571 square kilometers).

Two countries, two oceans, and a gulf form the boundaries of the United States. The countries are Canada and Mexico, the oceans are the Atlantic and the Pacific, and the gulf is the Gulf of Mexico.

The United States of America is made up of fifty states, plus the District of Columbia. Two of the states are separated from the other forty-eight. Alaska, the largest, is at the northwestern corner of the North American continent. Hawaii, a group of islands, is in the Pacific Ocean, over 2,000 miles from the west coast of North America. In addition, there are islands in the Pacific Ocean and Caribbean Sea known as the Outlying Territories. Because of the great distance from east to west, there are seven different time zones in the United States.

Compared with the rest of the world, the United States offers a high standard of living. The country's wealth is based on huge natural resources. These include coal, oil, gas, waterpower from great rivers, and iron ore. There are also large areas of very fertile soil.

Basic Geology and Structural Regions

The earth's continents all have a similar structure. One part of them is rigid and mostly flat. It has not changed very much over hundreds of millions of years. This part is called a *craton*. Around the craton are often long, narrow ranges of mountains, some with volcanoes. The edges of continents often slope quite steeply down to the ocean floor. Sometimes all of this steep continental shelf is entirely below water.

The great interior lowlands of the United States

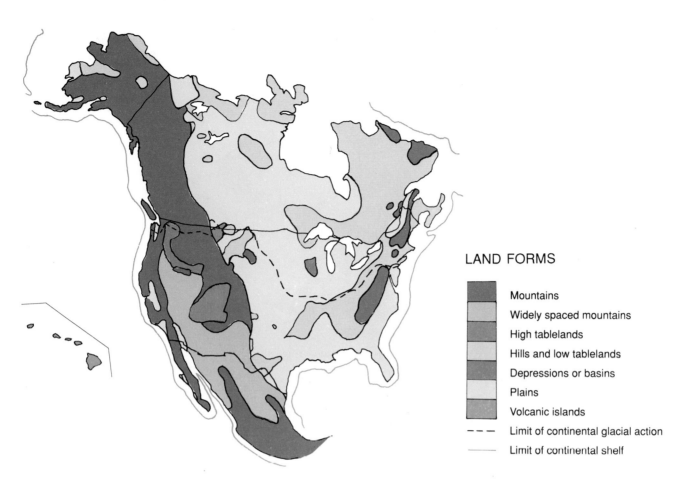

LAND FORMS

Mountains
Widely spaced mountains
High tablelands
Hills and low tablelands
Depressions or basins
Plains
Volcanic islands
- - - Limit of continental glacial action
——— Limit of continental shelf

are part of the craton of the North American continent. Most of this area is covered by relatively new rocks. But in the northern states, very ancient rocks can be seen at the surface.

The interior lowlands are drained by the Mississippi River and its tributaries (rivers and streams that flow into it). This is the third-largest river basin in the world. Only the Amazon and Congo basins are larger. The lowlands rise gradually to the west.

The western third of the United States is mountainous. There are two mountain ranges. The Sierra Nevada and the Cascades are close to the Pacific coast. The Rocky Mountains rise from the

Great Plains. Between the two ranges is a large plateau. In the north, mainly in Oregon and Idaho, is the Columbia Plateau. Toward the south, mainly in Utah, Arizona, and New Mexico, is the Colorado Plateau. One of its huge river gorges, the Grand Canyon, is over one mile (1.61 kilometers) deep in places.

The forces that make mountains are caused by constant movements in the earth's crust. The continents of the earth are moving very slowly on *plates* (large, partly rigid sections that can shift). These plates are created along mid-ocean ridges. When an ocean plate and a moving continent meet, the ocean plate pushes

under the continent. This folds, crushes, and lifts the rocks along the edge of the continent. The western mountains of the United States were formed in this way. Melted parts of the ocean plate sometimes push up and burst out onto the surface through volcanoes.

To the east of the interior lowlands are the Appalachian Mountains. This smaller and lower mountain range was created in a similar way to the western mountains. But the Appalachians started to form much longer ago – 800 million years rather than 150 million years – so the forces of erosion have had longer to wear them down.

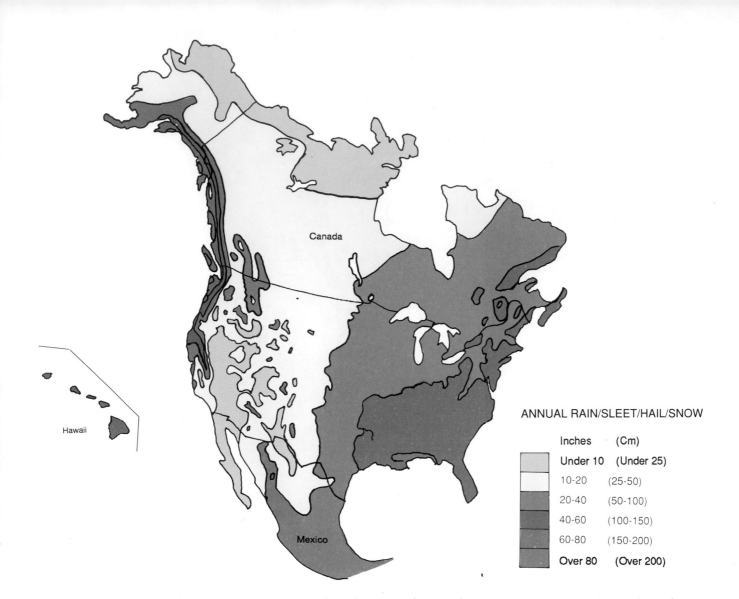

ANNUAL RAIN/SLEET/HAIL/SNOW

Inches	(Cm)
Under 10	(Under 25)
10-20	(25-50)
20-40	(50-100)
40-60	(100-150)
60-80	(150-200)
Over 80	(Over 200)

Along the southern and eastern edge of the United States are the Gulf and Atlantic coastal plains, which include the peninsula of Florida. These form an area of young, soft rocks. It slopes very gently down to the Gulf of Mexico and the Atlantic Ocean. About 50 to 150 miles offshore, it begins to fall away more steeply as the true edge of the continent is approached.

Weather always changes from day to day and, in some places, from hour to hour. Climate is the average weather measured over a very long period.

The climate of any place is affected by three things. First is the place's position on the earth's surface. The nearer it is to the *equator* (imaginary line around the middle of the earth), the hotter it will be. The nearer it is to the North or South Pole, the cooler it will be. The position of a place will also decide the direction of the winds and how much rain they may be carrying.

A second factor influencing the climate of a place is its nearness to the sea. The sea heats up and cools down more slowly than the land does. This means that places by the sea are warmer in winter and cooler in summer than inland areas. Places farther from the sea have more extreme climates: the summers are hotter and the winters are cooler. In such places, rainfall is likely to be heaviest in the summer months, when the heat causes thunderstorms to build up.

The third influence on climate is mountains. They can block the path of winds, forcing moist air upward. This air eventually cools and releases rain. Mountains are cooler than surrounding lowlands.

The United States (except Alaska) lies about halfway between the equator and the North Pole. This is a zone of temperate climate – not too hot and not too cold. The country can be divided roughly into a drier western half and a wetter eastern half. Moist winds from the Pacific Ocean are forced upward over the coastal mountains. Then the winds drop their rain on the western side of these mountains. This is the only area of very heavy rainfall in the west. As they blow into the mountain states, these winds, now dry, help to create areas of desert and semidesert.

To the east, rainfall increases again. Warm air from the Gulf of Mexico and the Atlantic Ocean carries moisture. Yearly rainfall, however, decreases inland and varies from 57 inches (145 centimeters) at New Orleans to 28 inches (71 centimeters) at Duluth.

Winter temperatures in the eastern part of the United States are influenced mainly by *latitude*, or how far north or south a place is. Tampa's average temperature for January is 60 degrees Fahrenheit (16 degrees Celsius), while Chicago's is 25 degrees Fahrenheit (minus 4 degrees Celsius). At this time of year, masses of very cold air have pushed south from Canada. Meanwhile, on the west coast, warm air is moving south from the northern Pacific Ocean. This keeps temperatures warmer than in the east.

In summer, hot, wet air from the Gulf of Mexico covers the whole of the country east of the Rocky Mountains. The difference in temperature between north and south is less in summer than in winter. Many thunderstorms are set off by the heat and humidity. On the west coast, the moist air of winter is replaced by drier winds. These keep the coast pleasantly cool and sometimes foggy. Inland, especially in the southwestern deserts, the sun shines through dry, cloudless air. Temperatures rise into the hundreds of degrees. The highest temperature ever recorded in the United States was 134 degrees Fahrenheit (57 degrees Celsius) in Death Valley, California.

The natural plant life of a country is determined mainly by its climate. But in many parts of the world – including the United States – the natural plant life has been changed or sometimes destroyed by human activity. So in some places, natural plant life means what *used* to grow before people planted crops, built cities, and made highways.

The natural plant life of the wetter, eastern half of the United States is mainly forest. In the extreme north, a narrow, broken belt of *coniferous* (cone-bearing) forest extends from Canada down through the Appalachians. Coniferous trees include pine, spruce, hemlock, and fir. In the extreme south – at the tip of Florida – there is

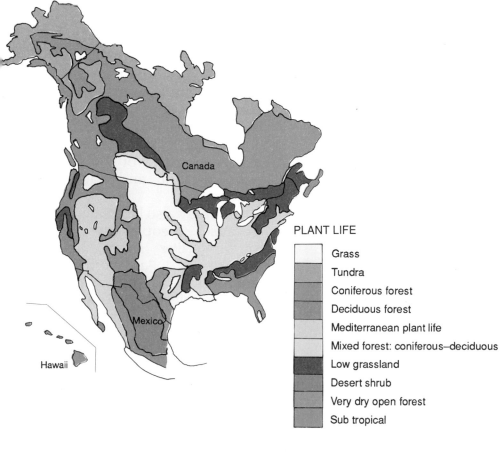

Canada

Mexico

Hawaii

PLANT LIFE

Grass
Tundra
Coniferous forest
Deciduous forest
Mediterranean plant life
Mixed forest: coniferous–deciduous
Low grassland
Desert shrub
Very dry open forest
Sub tropical

tropical plant life. Here, mangroves and palm trees grow. Between these two extremes, a great *deciduous* forest once stretched from New England to Minnesota and eastern Texas. Deciduous trees shed their leaves each year and include oak, ash, beech, maple, and sycamore.

West of the forested area, the grasslands formed a broad belt from Montana to New Mexico. They extended eastward into the central United States as far as Illinois. Much of this area has fertile soil and is very productive farmland.

In the mountainous west, plant life differs from place to place. Height above sea level and the amount of rainfall and sunlight all help to explain the differences. Coniferous forests cover many of the slopes of the coastal mountains. In the desert areas, cacti, yuccas, mesquite, and acacia grow. Sagebrush is common in the semidesert areas. The mountaintops have alpine (high-mountain) or tundra plant life. Small plants and shrubs that can flower quickly in the short growing season are found here.

The moist northwest coast has coniferous forests, which include Douglas fir and hemlock. In the south is the Californian *chaparral* with its scrubby, drought-resistant trees. Between these two areas are magnificent forests of sequoia, cypress, Douglas fir, and oak.

Population

A census is an official count of the people living in a country or area. Every ten years since 1790, a census has been taken of the United States. And each census has shown an increase in population from the one taken before.

By the end of the 1980s, for example, the United States had grown to about a quarter of a *billion* people. That's a huge jump from the 3,929,214 people living in the country in 1790. And it's an even bigger jump from the quarter of a *million* people estimated to have been living in the original thirteen colonies in the late 1600s.

The U.S. population is not evenly distributed across the country. The eastern half is more densely populated than the west where there are some nearly empty areas. The west coast, though is quite crowded.

Usually, people are attracted to places where they can make a good living for themselves and their families. Jobs may be there because of an abundance of natural resources such as iron ore, coal, or fertile soil. Or jobs may be there because of good transportation and trade links.

Jobs may also be created because people need services like shops or restaurants. And other areas of a country may force people away because of extreme weather or a lack of jobs.

All these forces influence the distribution of population in the United States.

Longs Peak in the Rocky Mountains of northern Colorado.

New York City, on the east coast, is one of the most densely populated cities in the United States.

There are two ways that a country's population can grow. When there are more births than deaths, there will be a natural increase. When more people are coming to live in a country (immigrants) than are leaving it (emigrants), the country will also experience growth. Both ways have contributed to increases in the U.S. population over the decades.

Until about 1860, almost all immigrants were from Great Britain, Germany, or Ireland (then wholly under the rule of Great Britain). In the final decades of the 1800s, waves of immigrants began coming from other European countries. During the twentieth century, many people have arrived from other North and South American countries and from Asia. Immigrants have many reasons for coming to the United States. Religious persecution, political problems, and lack of opportunity in their home country are among the chief ones.

Most black Americans also have their origins outside the country. A vast number are the descendants of African slaves. These slaves were brought to the original colonies and the United States between 1619 and 1865.

As immigrants arrived in the east and population grew steadily there, people started to move west to occupy new lands. The result was more frequent contact with the native peoples of the country: the American Indians. These contacts almost destroyed the Indian way of life. Indians were driven from their land and defeated in wars. More than half of all Indians now live on reservations (lands set aside for them by the U.S. Government).

Much of the west and southwest had been explored and settled by Spanish people. As the

The map below shows where the Indian nations were located in 1880. Inset is a portrait of Sitting Bull, the most famous of the Sioux Indians.

United States expanded westward, these people became part of the new country, too.

The United States has often been called a "melting pot." It means a place where people from many different cultures and races can come and blend into a new society.

The Northeast

The special features of this area are its great cities, including Boston, New York City, Philadelphia, Baltimore, and Washington, D.C. There are many more medium-sized cities and small towns as well. The Northeast is sometimes called a *megalopolis*, a term taken from two Greek words meaning "great city." It is a region made up of several large cities and their surrounding areas that are close enough together to be considered one big citylike area. At the heart of this megalopolis is New York City. Along with its surrounding areas, including Long Island and northeastern New Jersey, New York City is the largest metropolitan area in the world.

In some ways, it is surprising that there should be such big cities in the Northeast. The area does not have many natural resources. Soils are not fertile over most of the area, and there are few minerals. So why have these cities grown so large? The reason is partly historical and partly location. Washington, D.C., for

The United Nations Building in New York. Behind it are the skyscrapers of midtown Manhattan.

example, has grown because of its importance as the U.S. capital. The other four – Boston, New York City, Philadelphia, and Baltimore – were among the first cities set up by European colonists. They continued to be the points of entry for immigrants.

Moreover, they were key import and export centers for the colonies and for the growing United States. The cities were all connected to the interior by established routes. Each city also had an excellent harbor.

It is not surprising that there are some problems with such huge numbers of people living and working in these cities. The high cost of land, along with traffic, high crime rates, and pollution, can cause businesses and families to move out of the city center. Some move to the suburbs. Some leave

the region altogether for the better climate and more open spaces of the southern and western United States.

As people leave the city centers, there are fewer people left to pay the taxes. This means that some services needed by the whole city may have to be cut or cut back. Even with these problems, however, the cities of the northeast still dominate much of the country's business life.

The South

The states of the southeast are often grouped together under the name "the South." But in fact, it is a very varied area. Its landscapes include the gently sloping coastal plain as well as the rugged "ridge and valley" region of the Appalachian Mountains. Farming in the South also varies greatly from place to place. Sugar

The Big Cypress Swamp, with its tall trees, and the Everglades cover most of southern Florida.

cane, oranges, and grapefruit are grown in Florida. Tobacco is grown in North and South Carolina. Soybeans, cotton, and rice are farmed in the Mississippi Valley. Peaches are grown in Georgia and South Carolina. And peanuts and cotton are grown in Georgia and Alabama.

The South has a variety of valuable natural resources. These include coal, iron ore, bauxite (used in making aluminum), oil, and gas. There is plenty of electrical power. Much of the South is forested. About forty percent of the nation's trees are found here.

For a long time, the economy of the South depended heavily on farming. Cotton, the leading crop, was the main source of income. But since the 1950s, the South has undergone economic changes. Many of them stem from a dramatic increase in industry. Today, the South enjoys a better balance between farming, which is still important, and manufacturing.

The southernmost state in the continental United States is Florida. Citrus fruits are a leading state product, and tourism is a major state industry. Among Florida's popular attractions are Walt Disney World near Orlando, Cypress Gardens, and Everglades National Park.

The Central Plains

This area contains the two regions known as the Midwest and the Great Plains. They are noted for their great farming wealth and large industrial cities.

Different areas specialize in different kinds of farming. These areas are the great farming "belts." At their heart is the Corn Belt, stretching from Iowa to Ohio. It is one of the richest farming areas in the world. Farmers grow corn and soybeans, mainly for feeding to hogs and beef cattle.

To the north of the Corn Belt, steeper slopes, poorer soil, and colder winters encourage dairy farming. The Grain Belt takes over toward North and South Dakota and Kansas. The drier weather here is ideal for growing wheat. And Nebraska has huge ranches for cattle raising. Here, the land is sandy and generally not good for growing crops.

In the high plains near the Rocky Mountains, the climate becomes even drier. Cattle ranching is the main activity here. Crops can only be grown in the valleys where rivers provide water. This area of high plains stretches from western Texas to western North Dakota. To the south and east of the Corn Belt, conditions become less suitable for large-scale farming. The soil is often poorer and the landscape more rugged.

The other special feature of the Central Plains is its big industrial cities. The wealth of these cities comes from heavy manufacturing industries.

A wheat and hay harvest in eastern Colorado.

Nearly half the nation's iron and steel are made in the areas of Pittsburgh and Cleveland. Detroit and its surrounding towns make about two thirds of the nation's cars and trucks. Near the southern shore of Lake Michigan is the country's second-largest city, Chicago. Steel is made here and turned into many kinds of machines and equipment. The growth of industry in these cities has been helped by access to the Great Lakes. Ships can move materials easily and deliver them to where they are needed.

Other large industrial cities of the Central Plains are Cincinnati, St. Louis, Minneapolis, St. Paul, and Kansas City.

The West

Between the high plains and the Pacific coast lowlands lies a mountainous part of the United States. The wealth of the mountain states comes mainly from mining, farming, forestry, and

Chinatown and cable-cars are two major tourist attractions in cosmopolitan San Francisco.

The Golden Gate Bridge.

tourism. Many of the early settlers of this area were miners looking for gold. Today, mining is mainly for copper, zinc, lead, and silver.

Farming is difficult in the mountainous west. Mountain slopes are usually too steep, and the flatter areas between them are often too dry to support crops. The crops that are grown rely mostly on *irrigation*. This means taking water from rivers or wells and bringing it to the plants through pipes and sprinkler systems. Over most of the dry plateau areas, sheep and cattle ranching is the main activity.

Forestry (farming trees for their wood) and paper-making are important industries in western Montana, northern Idaho, Oregon, and Washington state. Sometimes, large areas are completely cut

down for timber before being replanted. Some people think that the trees should be cut down more gradually so that the landscape is not changed too much.

Millions of people visit the western United States each year. They come to explore the deserts and the Indian and Spanish parts of the southwest. They come to gaze at the magnificent mountain scenery and enjoy the warm, dry weather. They come to visit the natural wonders of the Grand Canyon, Yellowstone National Park, Yosemite National Park, and Death Valley. These visitors spend many millions of dollars in the region, making tourism an important industry here.

The Pacific coast, especially the coastal valleys of California, is a very rich farming area. Variations in climate allow many different crops to be grown. Cotton, grapes, oranges, lemons, grapefruits, peaches, pears, apricots, vegetables, barley, and rice are just some of them.

Industry has grown rapidly in California. Aerospace and electronics provide many jobs, and there is a big food processing industry here, too. The motion picture industry, based in Hollywood, has had worldwide impact. More people live in California than in any other state.

Hawaii

The state of Hawaii is a chain of 132 islands in the Pacific Ocean, about 2,400 miles (3,860 kilometers) from the coast of California. There are eight main islands: Hawaii, Kahoolawe, Kauai, Lanai, Maui, Molokai, Niihau, and Oahu. The rest are smaller, minor islands that have about three square miles (eight square kilometers) in total area.

The Hawaiian islands are actually the tops of Pacific floor volcanoes. Many of them are surrounded by coral reefs. Most of the volcanoes are dormant, but Mauna Loa and Kilauea on the island of Hawaii are still active. Although the eight main islands are in the tropics, they have a temperate climate. This is because of the cooling effect of the ocean. Winds from the northeast drop huge amounts of rain on the windward sides of the

islands. Mount Waialeale on Kauai is probably the wettest place on earth. It has an annual average rainfall of 460 inches (1,168 centimeters).

About eighty percent of Hawaiians live on the island of Oahu and forty percent live in the state capital, Honolulu. The population of the islands is mixed. It includes the original Polynesians, Japanese, Chinese, Filipinos, and Samoans.

Sandy beaches, warm weather, and spectacular volcanic scenery attract many visitors to Hawaii. Tourism is the state's main industry. Hawaii's economy also depends heavily on the U.S. military bases there, including Pearl Harbor. Pineapples

Harvesting pineapples in Hawaii. At night, the pickers work by lamplight.

and sugar cane are the state's leading crops. Hawaii grows more of these than any other state.

Alaska

Alaska is by far the largest state in the United States. Its area is 591,004 square miles (1,530,700 square kilometers). Alaska has huge mountain ranges.

The Brooks Range lies in the north and the Alaska Range in the south. There are active volcanoes and frequent earthquakes in the Alaska Range. This range includes North America's highest mountain, Mount McKinley, which is 20,320 feet (6,194 meters) high.

Alaska is a cold land. One third of the state lies inside the Arctic Circle. Much of Alaska is covered with Arctic tundra plant life: mosses, lichens, and low shrubs. These plants survive despite the very short summer thaw.

Alaska has one of the smallest populations of any state. Nearly half of its people live in and around Anchorage. About a sixth of the population are native peoples, including Eskimos and Aleuts.

Alaska is sometimes called America's "last frontier." This is because its great natural resources have not yet been fully developed. The state's leading mineral product is oil. Fishing (especially for salmon), forestry, and coal and gold mining are also important industries.

Outlying Territories

The United States owns thousands of islands scattered across the Pacific Ocean and the Caribbean Sea. Among them are Puerto Rico and the Virgin Islands in the Caribbean Sea, and American Samoa and Guam in the Pacific Ocean. The form of government often varies from island to island.

Our World

The earth is a very special place in our solar system. It is the only planet that has oceans, rivers, and an atmosphere that can support oxygen-using life forms. Also, temperatures on earth are fairly even, unlike the very hot and cold conditions found on other planets.

A Life-Supporting Planet

Life has been able to develop on earth because the physical environment has been just right for it. After the earth formed, the gases contained in its rocks escaped and cooled to form the first atmosphere and oceans. Conditions were then ready for the first life forms to develop in the early seas. Much later, plantlike cells that used carbon dioxide to make their food changed the original atmosphere by adding lots of oxygen to it. This enabled many different kinds of animals, including human beings, to develop.

The average temperature on the earth is about fifty-seven degrees Fahrenheit

(fourteen degrees Celsius). Temperatures on Mars range from −191 degrees Fahrenheit (−124 degrees Celsius) to −24 degrees Fahrenheit (−31 degrees Celsius). The mild temperature of the earth is one reason why it can support life.

Another reason why the earth can support life is that the air contains the right amounts of oxygen, carbon dioxide, and nitrogen. These gases are needed for the chemical processes common to all life forms on the earth.

The earth is covered mostly by water, and life cannot exist without it. Water forms a large part of the tissues of all plants and animals. And in the form of rivers and oceans, water has carved and shaped many of the earth's land features.

Land forms on the earth's surface range from plains and beaches to canyons and mountains.

The Earth's Zones

The earth is made up of a number of different zones, or circular layers, one inside the other. Some of these are solid, some are liquid, and some are gaseous. Surrounding the solid earth is a layer of various gases called the atmosphere. In total, the atmosphere is about 1,000 miles (1,600 kilometers) deep. The lowest part is called the troposphere. It is made up mainly of the gases nitrogen, oxygen, carbon dioxide, water vapor, and others. This layer is about seven miles (eleven kilometers) thick. All the physical events that cause our weather take place in the troposphere.

Above the troposphere lies the stratosphere, which is thin, almost cloudless air. The stratosphere contains the ozone layer, which is at risk today from pollution. Ozone is made up of oxygen atoms arranged differently from those found in ordinary oxygen gas. The ozone layer is important to all life forms because it absorbs many of the harmful rays from the sun.

The highest layer is called the ionosphere. This layer causes radio waves sent up from the earth to bounce back to the ground, permitting radio programs to be sent around the world.

The atmosphere is held close to the earth by gravity, the force that pulls things toward the earth's center. The atmosphere is densest, or thickest, close to the earth's surface. People who climb high mountains must wear oxygen masks to help them breathe. This is because the air thins out and contains less oxygen as they climb higher and higher.

Below the atmosphere are the earth's continents and oceans. For convenience, all the water in the earth's seas and rivers is considered one zone. This zone is called the hydrosphere, which means "zone of water." The land of continents and ocean bottoms forms the surface of the topmost solid layer of the earth. This layer is the zone called the lithosphere. It extends to a depth ranging from 40 miles (65 kilometers) to 90 miles (145 kilometers) below the surface.

The biosphere includes land, water, and even part of the atmosphere. The name means "zone of life." The biosphere contains all the living things on land, in water, and in the air.

Water, Water Everywhere

The earth's surface is about seventy percent water. This is an area equal to 139,692,000 square miles (361,800,000 square kilometers). The land area of the earth is only 57,259,000 square miles (148,300,000 square kilometers).

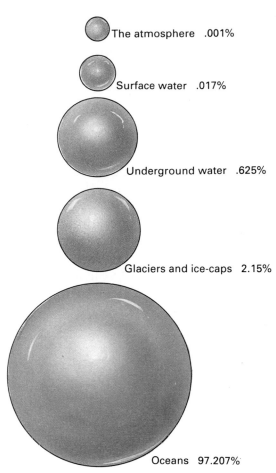

The atmosphere .001%

Surface water .017%

Underground water .625%

Glaciers and ice-caps 2.15%

Oceans 97.207%

This shows where the earth's water comes from.

Facts and Figures

The earth is not perfectly round. It bulges slightly at the equator, the imaginary line running around the middle of the earth. Because of this bulge, the diameter (distance straight through) of the earth is 7,900 miles (12,700 kilometers) at the poles and 7,925 miles (12,750 kilometers) at the equator. The distance around the earth at the equator is 24,900 miles (40,100 kilometers).

The central core of the earth is thought to be made mostly of iron, with some nickel. But nobody really knows for sure.

The Anatomy of the Earth

For thousands of years, people have wondered what is inside the earth. Only recently has it been possible to get some idea of what the earth might look like inside. We know the most about the earth's outer skin, the crust, because that is where we live. It is also where events occur that most directly affect us, such as earthquakes and volcanic eruptions. These happen because of disturbances far below the surface of the earth.

The Age of the Earth

Hundreds of years ago, people thought that the earth was only a few thousand years old. Modern geologists study rocks, fossils, and other features to learn the earth's true age. They can use accurate dating methods based on the fact that rocks contain radioactive elements, those that change over time into other elements. Rocks containing these radioactive elements give the geologists clues as to how much time has passed since the rocks were first formed. The earth is now thought to be about 4.6 billion years old.

Earthquake Waves

We know about the inside of the earth mostly through earthquakes. Shock waves from earthquakes either travel through or are reflected by the materials of the various shells that make up the earth. These waves are recorded by an instrument called a seismograph. Some types of waves can travel only through liquid matter. Others travel through both liquids and solids. The speed of the waves also varies. The paths and speed of earthquake waves moving through the interior of the earth give scientists clues about the make-up of the earth's various shells.

Four types of rock used in radioactive dating: pitchblende, orangite, orthoclase, and torbernite.

The division of the earth's layers between the crust and the mantle was discovered in 1909. Next to be identified was the division between the mantle and core. Geologists believe that the core is liquid outside and solid in the center.

Depth of the Crust

The crust of the earth differs in depth, depending on whether it forms an ocean bottom or a continent. Under the oceans, the crust is about five miles (eight kilometers) thick. Continental crust ranges from twenty-one miles (thirty-four kilometers) to twenty-five miles (forty kilometers) in thickness.

The crust forming the continent consists of different types of rock. The crust beneath the oceans, however, is simpler.

The solid crust and the solid topmost layer of the mantle "float" on a partially liquid zone of the mantle. The solid floating double layer (the lithosphere) is broken up into separate large **plates** that rub up and collide against each other. Where these

This volcano in Mexico, called Paracutín, erupted spectacularly in 1943. The lava peak grew to 450 feet (137 meters) in only 2 weeks.

Inside the earth

Crust

Mantle

Outer core

Inner core

plates shift and collide, earthquakes occur. The San Andreas Fault in California is such a place. When these shifts occur underwater, chains of volcanic islands and underwater volcanoes form.

This diagram shows how chains of volcanic islands are formed where one plate slides beneath another.

A geologist tests a rock sample drilled from the ocean floor.

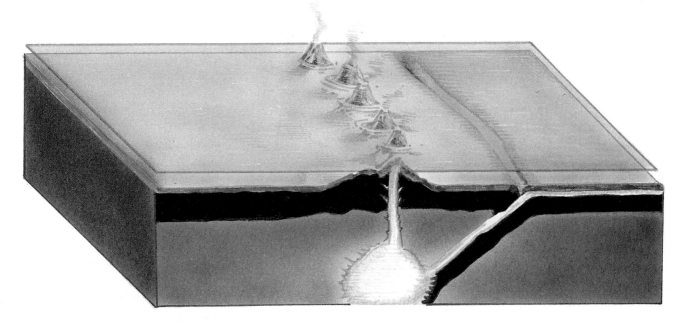

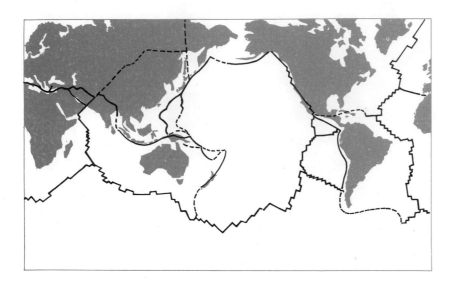

The crust of the earth is thought to consist of about fifteen plates. The black jagged lines show where the boundaries probably are. Where the plates meet, earthquakes and volcanoes occur.

Movements and Activity

The surface of the earth is constantly worn away by water and wind. But the earth has not become smooth and flat. In fact, some mountains are nearly 30,000 feet (9,150 meters) high. Obviously, there must be forces that work against those wearing away the land.

Sometimes material is forced upward, creating volcanoes, islands, and mountain ranges. In other areas, the plates slide past each other.

It is believed that the plates move by convection currents, forces set up by different temperatures within the mantle. This causes currents to rise. When they reach the upper part of the mantle, they cool and sink down again. All of this creates a stirring action, which shifts the plates and also forces out new molten material.

Drifting Continents

If you look at a map of the world, you will see that the coastlines of Africa and South America would fit very nearly together like pieces in a jigsaw puzzle. This is because at one time, they were joined together.

The earth's rigid top layer is thought to be broken up into about fifteen jigsawlike pieces called plates. These plates float on a partly molten layer of the mantle underneath them. Some of the plates carry only oceanic crust; others also carry continental crust. When these plates move apart, they separate any landmasses on top. When the plates push against each other, the landmasses rising on top collide and cause the edges of the land to buckle up into mountain ranges.

Folded Rocks

Sediment is usually deposited in horizontal layers. Over billions of years, the movement of the plates folds, buckles, and breaks the layers of sediment into new forms.

When rocks are folded into an arch, they form what is called an anticline. When they are folded to form a basin, the structure is called a syncline.

Some folding is very small, while some is on a very large scale. Portions of such mountain ranges as the Alps, the Himalayas, the Rockies, and the Appalachians are made up of folded rocks.

Faults

Under the great pressure of shifting plates, layers of rocks may crack apart rather than fold. Such a crack or split between two masses of rock is known as a fault. Movement along faults is the cause of earthquakes.

The San Andreas Fault, which runs through California, is probably the most famous one in the world. It marks the edges of the Pacific plate and the North American plate, and it was responsible for the San Francisco earthquakes of 1906 and 1989.

Influences on the Earth's Surfaces

The Cycle of Erosion

The surface of the earth is constantly under attack. The scenery you see around you today is actually built on the wreckage of former worlds. The breaking up of rocks on the surface and their movement to other places is called erosion. The effects of the weather, called weathering, are part of the process of erosion.

Rain plays a large part in erosion, especially where there is little plant cover to hold the topsoil together. Rain washes out soil to form gullies and deep, narrow valleys. It also seeps into rock cracks, gradually loosening and splitting the rocks. Expanding ice, changes in temperature, chemical reactions in air and water, and plants and burrowing animals all act to break up soil and rock on the earth's surface.

In mountain areas affected by ice, there are often large piles of broken rock. This material is called scree. Here, winds also scour rocks and carry away loose soil.

Glaciers (slowly moving masses of ice) and running water also erode the earth's surface. Glaciers carry broken rocks from

Rivers play a major part in the process of erosion. They move large amounts of broken-up rock and finer material from one place to another. Where rivers are fast-flowing, they can carve deep valleys and canyons in the rocks of the earth's surface.

place to place. The force of water from rivers, streams, rainstorms, and floods wears down the surface of the land. In addition, the water carries small particles of rock, called sediment, and deposits it far away.

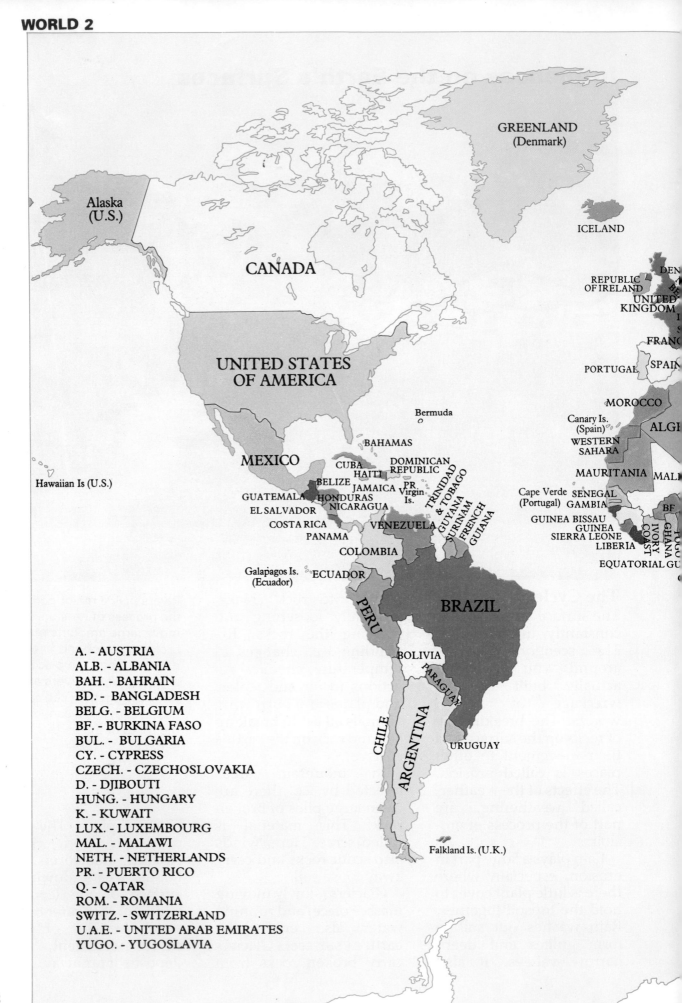

GREENLAND
(Denmark)

Alaska
(U.S.)

ICELAND

CANADA

REPUBLIC
OF IRELAND
DEN

UNITED
KINGDOM

FRANC

SPAIN

PORTUGAL

UNITED STATES
OF AMERICA

MOROCCO

Bermuda

Canary Is.
(Spain)

ALG

WESTERN
SAHARA

MEXICO

BAHAMAS

DOMINICAN
REPUBLIC

CUBA
HAITI

MAURITANIA

MAL

Hawaiian Is (U.S.)

BELIZE
JAMAICA

PR.
Virgin
Is.

TRINIDAD
& TOBAGO

Cape Verde
(Portugal)

SENEGAL

GAMBIA

GUATEMALA
HONDURAS

GUINEA BISSAU

BF

EL SALVADOR
NICARAGUA

GUYANA

SURINAM

FRENCH
GUIANA

GUINEA

TOGO

COSTA RICA

VENEZUELA

SIERRA LEONE

IVORY
COAST

GHANA

PANAMA

LIBERIA

COLOMBIA

EQUATORIAL GU

Galapagos Is.
(Ecuador)

ECUADOR

BRAZIL

PERU

BOLIVIA

PARAGUAY

CHILE

ARGENTINA

URUGUAY

Falkland Is. (U.K.)

A. - AUSTRIA
ALB. - ALBANIA
BAH. - BAHRAIN
BD. - BANGLADESH
BELG. - BELGIUM
BF. - BURKINA FASO
BUL. - BULGARIA
CY. - CYPRESS
CZECH. - CZECHOSLOVAKIA
D. - DJIBOUTI
HUNG. - HUNGARY
K. - KUWAIT
LUX. - LUXEMBOURG
MAL. - MALAWI
NETH. - NETHERLANDS
PR. - PUERTO RICO
Q. - QATAR
ROM. - ROMANIA
SWITZ. - SWITZERLAND
U.A.E. - UNITED ARAB EMIRATES
YUGO. - YUGOSLAVIA

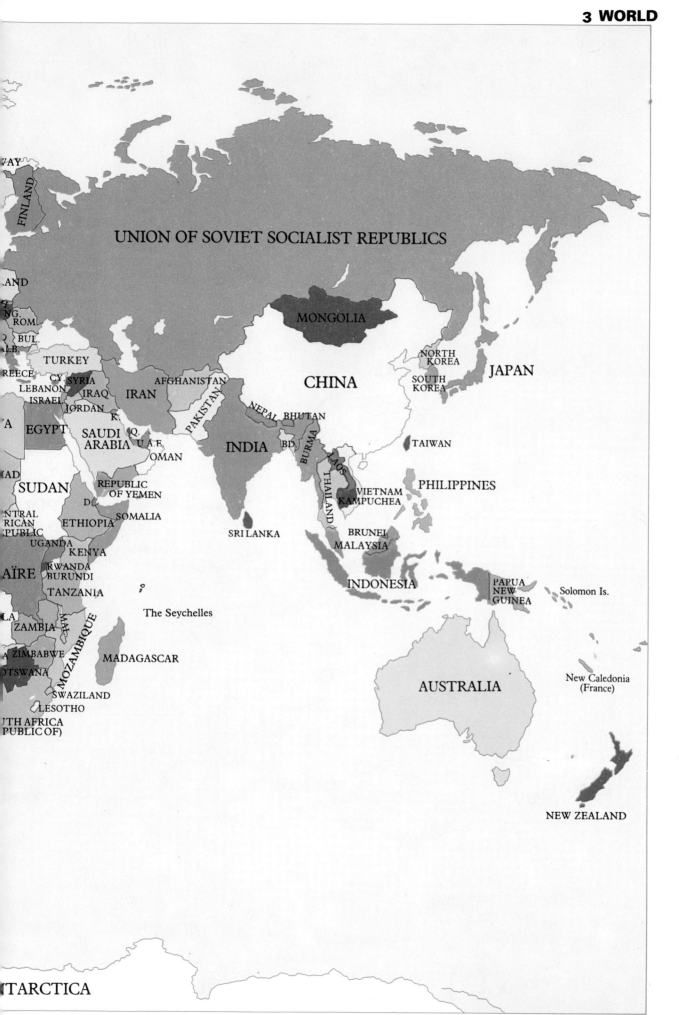

UNION OF SOVIET SOCIALIST REPUBLICS

FINLAND

VAY

AND

NG.
ROM.
BUL.
ALB.
GREECE
TURKEY
CY.
LEBANON SYRIA
ISRAEL
JORDAN IRAQ
EGYPT
SAUDI
ARABIA
Q.
U.A.E.
OMAN
SUDAN
REPUBLIC
OF YEMEN
D.
NTRAL
RICAN
PUBLIC
ETHIOPIA
SOMALIA
UGANDA
KENYA
AÏRE
RWANDA
BURUNDI
TANZANIA
A
ZAMBIA
MOZAMBIQUE
MADAGASCAR
ZIMBABWE
TSWANA
SWAZILAND
LESOTHO
TH AFRICA
PUBLIC OF)

MONGOLIA

AFGHANISTAN

IRAN

PAKISTAN

NEPAL BHUTAN
INDIA BD.
BURMA

K.

CHINA

NORTH
KOREA
SOUTH
KOREA

JAPAN

TAIWAN

LAOS
THAILAND
VIETNAM
KAMPUCHEA

PHILIPPINES

SRI LANKA

BRUNEI
MALAYSIA

INDONESIA

The Seychelles

PAPUA
NEW
GUINEA

Solomon Is.

New Caledonia
(France)

AUSTRALIA

NEW ZEALAND

NEW ZEALAND

TARCTICA

65°

A   B   C   D   E

ARCTIC

ICELAND   Arctic Circle

30°

N O R W E G I A N   S E A

miles
0   100   200   300

0   200   400   600
kilometers

Galdhøppigen
8110'
(2469)

55°

NORWAY

SWEDEN

ATLANTIC

OCEAN

Ben Nevis
4406'
(1343m)

N O R T H

S E A

20°

DENMARK
Jutland

BALTIC
SE

IRELAND   UNITED
KINGDOM

NETHERLANDS

POLAN

North

GERMANY

Oder

Thames

45°

English Channel

BELGIUM

LUXEMBOURG

Rhine

Elbe

Danube

CZECHOSLOVA

Seine

Loire

FRANCE   SWITZERLAND

LIECHTENSTEIN

AUSTRIA   Hung

HUNG

Bay of
Biscay

MASSIF

CENTRAL

Rhône

Mt Blanc
15,781'
(4807m)

Po

DINARIC AL

Garonne

CANTABRIAN
MTS

Duero

PYRÉNÉES

ANDORRA

MONACO

LIGURIAN
SEA

ITALY   SAN MARINO

Sa

PORTUGAL

Meseta

Ebro

Pico de Aneto
11,168'
(3404m)

APENNINES

ADRIATIC

SEA

YUGOSI

Tagus

SPAIN

AL

Guadiana

Guadalquivir

SIERRA
NEVADA

TYRRHENIAN
SEA

ION
S

35°

Strait of Gibraltar

M E D I T E R R A N E A N

Mt Etna
10,705'
(3340m)

ATLAS MTS

S E A

80   10°

MOROCCO

ALGERIA

TUNISIA

MALTA

0°   10°

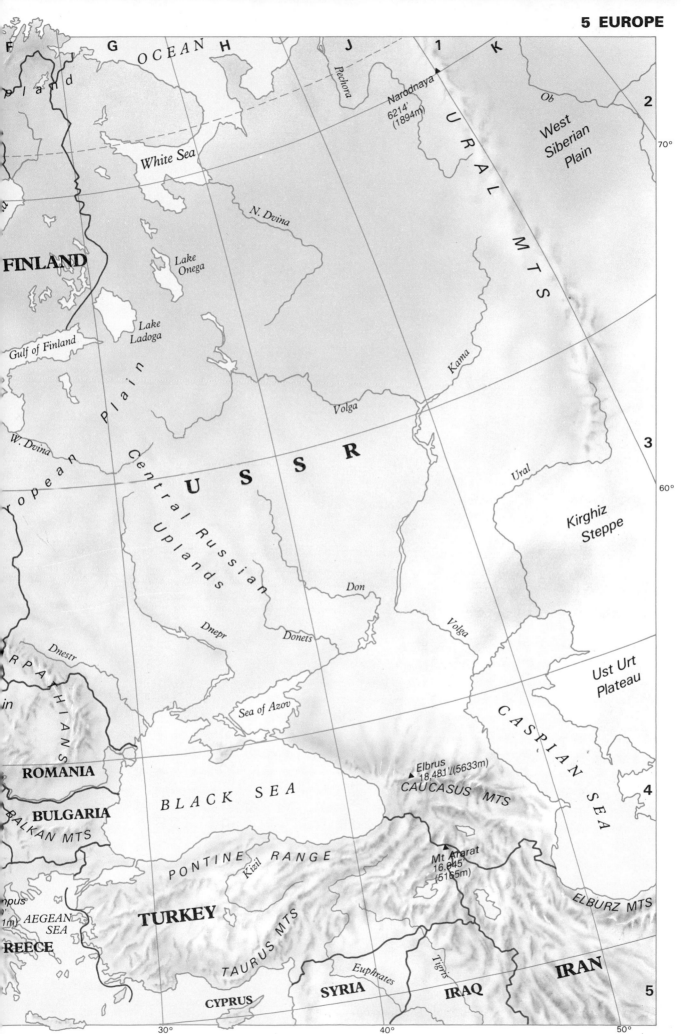

F   G   OCEAN   H   J   1   K

Pechora

West
Siberian
Plain

2

70°

Narodnaya
6214'
(1894m)

White Sea

U
R
A
L

M
T
S

Ob

N. Dvina

Lake
Onega

FINLAND

Lake
Ladoga

P
l
a
i
n

C
e
n
t
r
a
l

Volga

Kama

Gulf of Finland

W. Dvina

U S S R

Ural

3

60°

Kirghiz
Steppe

C
e
n
t
r
a
l

R
u
s
s
i
a
n

U
p
l
a
n
d
s

Don

Volga

Ust Urt
Plateau

Dnestr

Dnepr

Donets

Sea of Azov

C
A
S
P
I
A
N

RPATHIANS

in

ROMANIA

Elbrus
18,481'(5633m)

CAUCASUS   MTS

S
E
A

4

BULGARIA

BLACK   SEA

ALKAN MTS

PONTINE   RANGE

Kizil

Mt Ararat
16,945'
(5165m)

npus

AEGEAN
SEA

1m)

REECE

TURKEY

TAURUS MTS

Euphrates

Tigris

ELBURZ MTS

IRAN

CYPRUS   SYRIA   IRAQ

5

30°   40°   50°

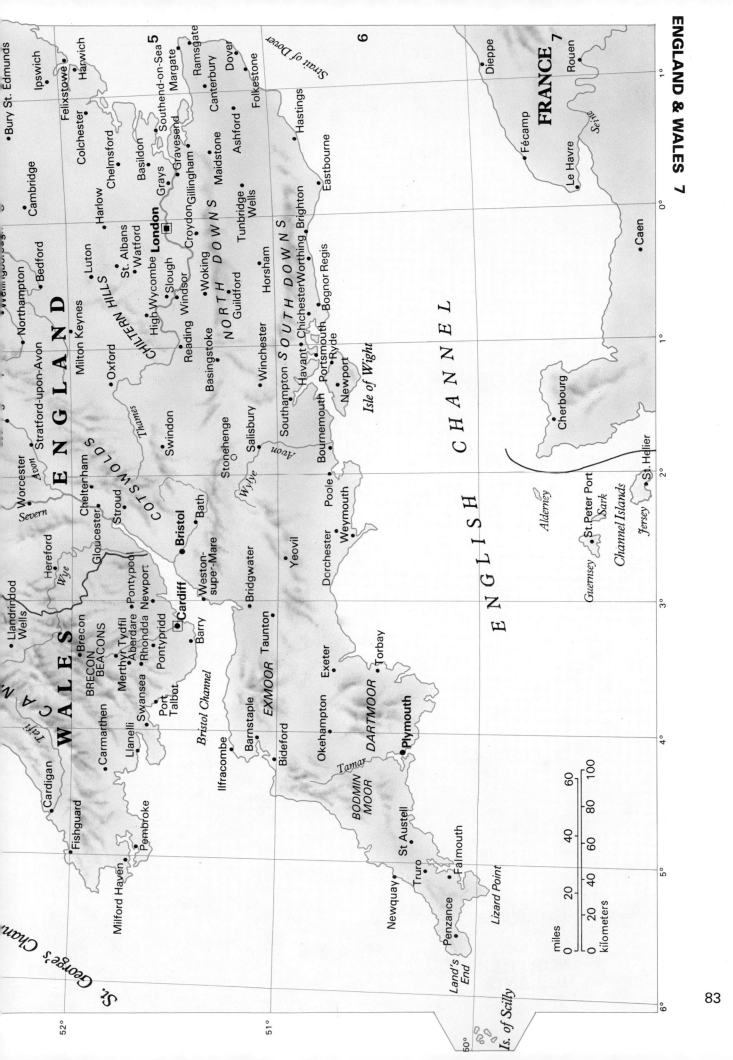

ENGLAND

WALES

FRANCE 7

NORTH DOWNS

SOUTH DOWNS

CHILTERN HILLS

COTSWOLDS

BRECON BEACONS

EXMOOR

DARTMOOR

BODMIN MOOR

ENGLISH CHANNEL

Strait of Dover

St. George's Channel

Bristol Channel

Channel Islands

Isle of Wight

Bury St. Edmunds
Ipswich
Felixstowe
Harwich
Cambridge
Colchester
Chelmsford
Bedford
Harlow
Basildon
Luton
Grays
Southend-on-Sea 5
Milton Keynes
St. Albans
Watford
Slough
Gravesend
Margate
Ramsgate
Northampton
Stratford-upon-Avon
Oxford
High Wycombe
London
Croydon Gillingham
Canterbury
Dover
Folkestone
Worcester
Cheltenham
Swindon
Reading
Windsor
Woking
Maidstone
Ashford
Hastings
Hereford
Gloucester
Stroud
Bath
Basingstoke
Guildford
Tunbridge Wells
Brighton
Eastbourne
Cardiff
Bristol
Weston-super-Mare
Stonehenge
Salisbury
Winchester
Horsham
Chichester Worthing
Bognor Regis
Llandrindod Wells
Brecon
Newport
Barry
Bridgwater
Yeovil
Southampton
Havant
Portsmouth
Ryde
Bournemouth
Poole
Weymouth
Dorchester
Newport
Merthyr Tydfil
Aberdare
Rhondda
Pontypridd
Pontypool
Taunton
Carmarthen
Swansea
Port Talbot
Barnstaple
Bideford
Exeter
Torbay
Llanelli
Ilfracombe
Okehampton
Plymouth
Cardigan
Fishguard
Pembroke
Milford Haven
St Austell
Truro
Falmouth
Newquay
Penzance
Land's End
Lizard Point
Is. of Scilly
Dieppe
Rouen
Le Havre
Fécamp
Caen
Cherbourg
Alderney
Guernsey
St. Peter Port
Sark
Jersey
St. Helier

Severn
Wye
Teifi
Thames
Avon
Wylye
Avon
Tamar
Seine

83

Shetland Islands

Lerwick

at same scale

ATLANTIC OCEAN

NORTH SEA

Fair Isle

Orkney Islands

Kirkwall

Pentland Firth

John O'Groats

Thurso

Wick

OUTER HEBRIDES

Stornoway

Lewis

Helmsdale

Loch Shin

Lairg

Harris

Tarbert

Ullapool

NORTH WEST HIGHLANDS

Moray Firth

Banff

Fraserburgh

North Uist

Portree

Stromeferry

Cromarty

Dingwall

Nairn

Elgin

Keith

Huntly

Peterhead

Skye

Kyle of Lochalsh

Inverness

Grantown-on-Spey

South Uist

Broadford

Spey

Don

Aberdeen

Eriskay

Rhum

GLENMORE

Loch Ness

Dee

Barra

CAIRNGORMS

Ben Macdhui 4296' (1311m)

Ballater

Braemar

Stonehaven

Eigg

Fort William

Ben Nevis 4406' (1343m)

GRAMPIAN MOUNTAINS

Brechin

Montrose

Coll

Pitlochry

Forfar

INNER HEBRIDES

Tiree

Mull

Oban

Tay

Loch Tay

Dundee

Arbroath

SCOTLAND

Perth

Firth of Tay

St. Andrews

Firth of Lorn

Callander

Glenrothes

Jura

Loch Lomond

Stirling

Kirkcaldy

Firth of Forth

Dunfermline

Dunbar

Dumbarton

Cumbernauld

Falkirk

Edinburgh

Clydebank

Greenock

Glasgow

Paisley

Coatbridge

Berwick-upon-Tweed

Islay

Bute

Hamilton

Motherwell

Wishaw

Peebles

East Kilbride

Galashiels

Tweed

Arran

Irvine

Kilmarnock

Clyde

SOUTHERN UPLANDS

Firth of Clyde

Ayr

Prestwick

Moffat

Hawick

Campbeltown

North Channel

Girvan

Portrush

Dumfries

ENGLAND

Coleraine

NORTHERN IRELAND (U.K.)

Newton Stewart

Londonderry

Ballymena

Larne

Stranraer

Solway Firth

Carlisle

miles
0   20   40   60

0 20 40 60 80 100
kilometers

59°

60°

58°

57°

56°

55°

1°

7°   6°   5°   4°   3°   2°

A   B   C   D   E   F   G

1

2

3

4

5

6

miles
0   20   40   60
0 20 40 60 80 100
kilometers

A B C D E F

North Channel

ATLANTIC OCEAN

Portrush
Ballycastle
Buncrana
Coleraine
Lough Foyle
Londonderry
Larne
Bann
Ballymena
Strabane
NORTHERN IRELAND
Antrim
Belfast Lough
Newtownabbey
Bangor
(U.K.)
☐ **Belfast**
Donegal
Omagh
Lough Neagh
Lisburn
Ballyshannon
Portadown
Lurgan
Donegal Bay
Lower Lough Erne
Enniskillen
Armagh
Downpatrick
Sligo
Monaghan
Newry
Upper Lough Erne
Ballina
Carrickmacross
Dundalk
Lough Conn
Carrick-on-Shannon

IRISH

Achill Isle
Castlebar
Longford
Kells
SEA
Westport
Drogheda
Roscommon
Lough Mask
REPUBLIC OF IRELAND
3
Lough Corrib
Lough Ree
Clifden
Athlone
Dublin Howth
Athenry
Clara
Liffey
Galway
Ballinasloe
Dun Laoghaire
Galway Bay
Shannon
Naas
Kildare
Aran Is
Portlaoighise
Wicklow
Lough Derg
Roscrea
Athy
Kilkee
Ennis
Nenagh
Carlow
Arklow
Barrow
Kilrush
Thurles
Kilkenny
Limerick
Cashel
WICKLOW MTS
Tipperary
Tralee
Clonmel
New Ross
Wexford
Waterford
Blackwater
Dingle
Killarney
Dungarvan
Dingle Bay
Mallow
Youghal
▲ Carrauntoohill
3406'
(1041m) Kenmare
Cork
Bandon
Cobh
Bantry
Bantry Bay

St. George's Channel

10°   9°   8°   7°   6°

A B C D

ENGLAND

Southampton
Exeter Bournemouth Portsmouth Brighton
Plymouth • • Do
Penzance • Torbay Isle of Wight
• Truro

50° *English Channel*

Alderney Dieg

Guernsey *Sark* Cherbourg Le Havre
Channel Islands • R
Br. *Jersey* Caen •
St. Helier

Alençon •
Île d'Ouessant • Morlaix St. Malo
Brest • • Fougères
St. Brieuc • Rennes
48° Quimper •

Le Mans •
Lorient •

Vannes **F**
•

Belle Île St. Nazaire *Loire* Angers Tours
• •

Nantes • Cholet

Île de Noirmoutier Châtellerault •

Île d'Yeu • La Roche- Poitiers
sur-Yon •

46° *Île de Ré*

Île d'Oléron

Bay *of* Cognac Limo
• Angoulême
Biscay •

Gironde Périgue
•

miles
0 50 100 Bergerac
0 50 100 150 Bordeaux *Dordogne*
kilometers •

44°

Agen
•

Gulf of Gascony Montau

Dax *Adour*
• Toulo
Gijón Santander
• • Biarritz Bayonne
Oviedo Torrelavega • • Pau Tarbes
• • Bilbao • •
San Sebastián Lourdes
S P A I N Vitoria **PYRÉNÉ**
• Pamplona Pic de
Vignemale Pico de Aneto
10,821'(3298m) 11,168'(3404m)

6° 4° 2° 0°

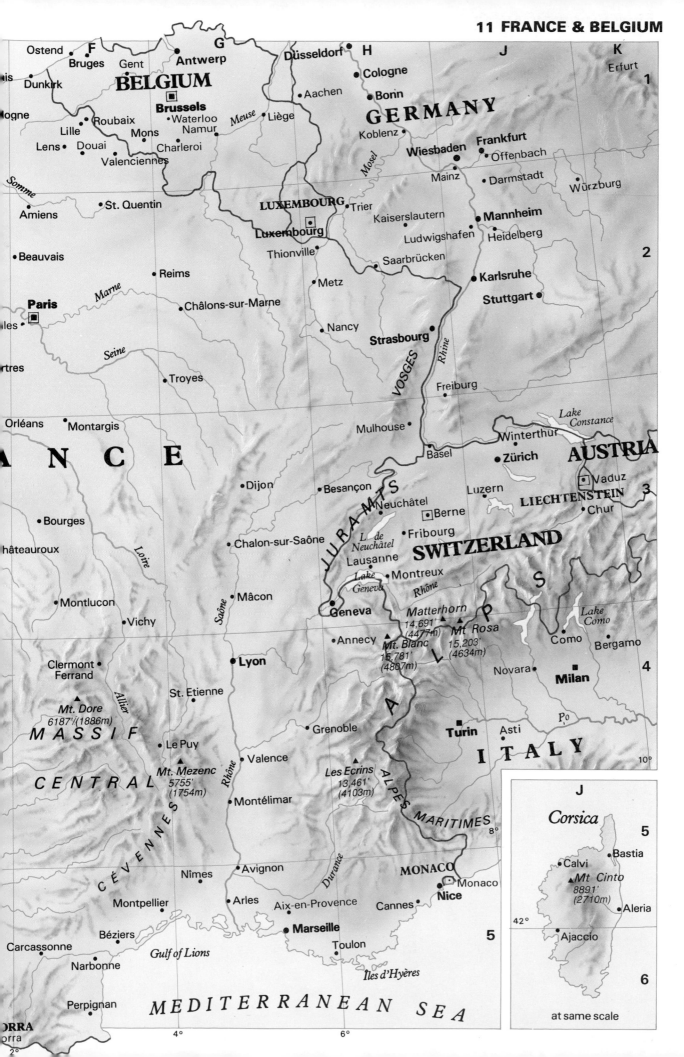

Ostend · F · G · Düsseldorf · H · J · K
Bruges · Gent · Antwerp · Cologne · Erfurt 1
Dunkirk · **BELGIUM** · Aachen · Bonn · **GERMANY**
les · Roubaix · Waterloo · Liège · Koblenz
Lille · Mons · Namur · Charleroi · Wiesbaden · Frankfurt · Offenbach · Würzburg
Lens · Douai · Valenciennes · Mainz · Darmstadt
· St. Quentin · **LUXEMBOURG** · Trier · Kaiserslautern · **Mannheim** · Heidelberg
· Beauvais · **Luxembourg** · Thionville · Ludwigshafen · Saarbrücken · **Karlsruhe** · Stuttgart 2
· Reims · Metz · **Stuttgart**
Paris · Châlons-sur-Marne · Nancy · **Strasbourg**
les · Seine · Troyes · Freiburg · VOSGES · Rhine
Chartres
Orléans · Montargis · Lake Constance
A N C E · Dijon · Besançon · Mulhouse · Winterthur · **AUSTRIA** · Vaduz 3
· Bourges · Basel · Zürich · LIECHTENSTEIN · Chur
âteauroux · Chalon-sur-Saône · Neuchâtel · Berne · Luzern
· L. de Neuchâtel · Fribourg · **SWITZERLAND** · S
Montluçon · Mâcon · Lausanne · Montreux · P
· Vichy · Lake Geneva · Rhône · Lake Como
Geneva · Matterhorn · Mt Rosa · Como · Bergamo
Clermont Ferrand · Annecy · 14,691' (4477m) · 15,203' (4634m) · L · Novara · **Milan** 4
Mt. Dore · St. Etienne · **Lyon** · Mt. Blanc 15,781' (4807m) · Po · Asti
6187'/(1886m) · Le Puy · Grenoble · **Turin** · **I T A L Y** 10°
M A S S I F · Mt. Mezenc 5755' (1754m) · Valence · Les Ecrins 13,461' (4103m) · ALPES
C E N T R A L · Montélimar · MARITIMES · 8°
Nîmes · Avignon · Durance · **MONACO** 5
Montpellier · Arles · Aix-en-Provence · Monaco
Béziers · Cannes · **Nice**
Carcassonne · **Marseille** · Toulon
Narbonne · Gulf of Lions · Îles d'Hyères
Perpignan · **M E D I T E R R A N E A N   S E A** 87
rra · 2° · 4° · 6°

J
Corsica 5
· Bastia
· Calvi
▲ *Mt Cinto* 8891' (2710m)
· Aleria 6
42°
· Ajaccio
at same scale

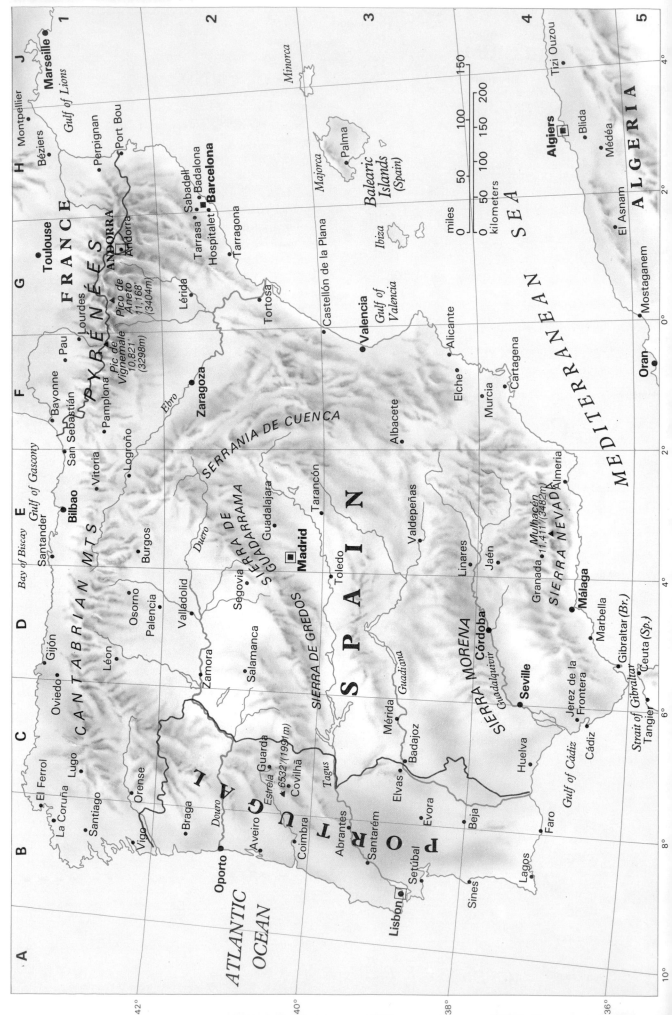

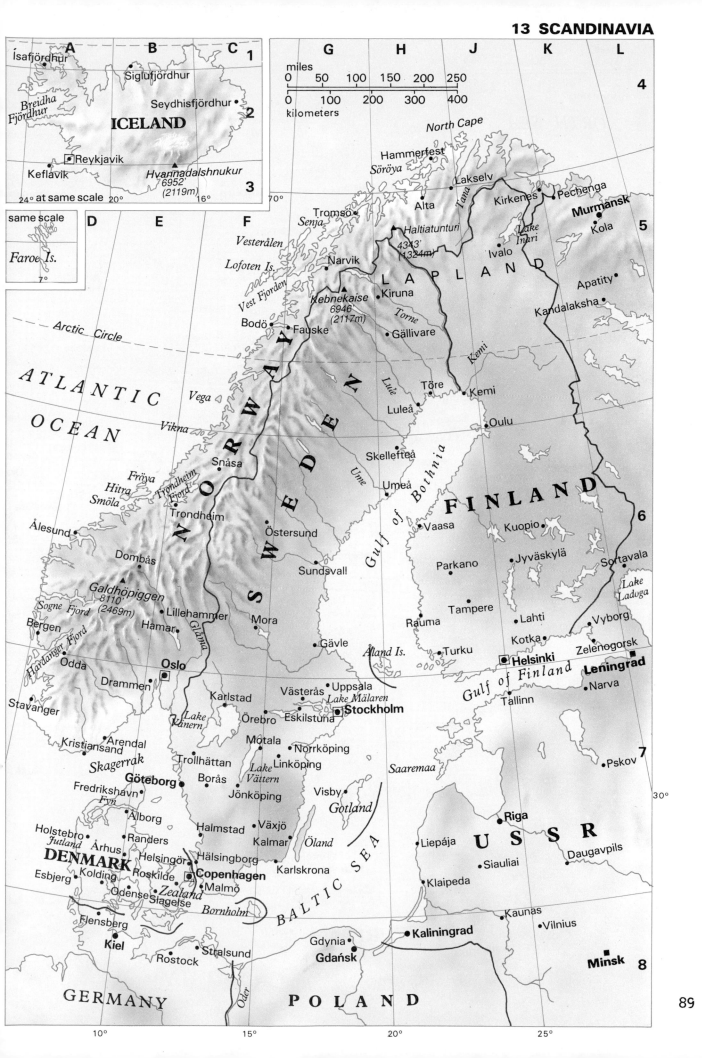

A · B · C · 1

Ísafjördhur

Breidha
Fjördhur

Siglufjördhur

Seydhisfjördhur · 2

ICELAND

Keflavik

⊡ Reykjavik

Hvannadalshnukur
6952'
(2119m) ▲ · 3

24° at same scale · 20° · 16°

same scale

D · E · F

Faroe Is.

7°

miles
0 50 100 150 200 250
0 100 200 300 400
kilometers

North Cape

G · H · J · K · L · 4

Hammerfest
Söröya

Lakselv

Kirkenes · Pechenga

Murmansk

Alta

Tana

Kola

70°

Tromsö
Senja

Haltiatunturi
4343'
(1324m) ▲

Ivalo

*Lake
Inari*

Apatity · 5

Vesterålen

Lofoten Is.

Narvik

L A P L A N D

Kandalaksha

Vest Fjorden

Kebnekaise
6946'
(2117m) ▲

Kiruna

Bodö

Fauske

Torne

Gällivare

Kemi

Arctic   Circle

Vega

Lule

Töre

Kemi

A T L A N T I C

Vikna

Luleå

Oulu

O C E A N

Skellefteå

Snåsa

Fröya

Hitra

Smöla

*Trondheim
Fjord*

Trondheim

Östersund

Ume

Umeå

Gulf of Bothnia

F I N L A N D

Vaasa

Kuopio

6

Ålesund

Dombås

Sundsvall

Parkano

Jyväskylä

Sortavala

Galdhöpiggen
8110'
(2469m) ▲

Lillehammer

Sogne Fjord

Mora

Tampere

*Lake
Ladoga*

Bergen

Hamar

Glåma

Gävle

Rauma

Lahti

Vyborg

Hardanger Fjord

Odda

Åland Is.

Turku

Kotka

Zelenogorsk

Stavanger

Drammen

⊡ **Oslo**

Karlstad

Västerås

Uppsala

Lake Mälaren

⊡ **Helsinki**

Leningrad ■

Gulf of Finland

Narva

Kristiansand

Arendal

*Lake
Vänern*

Örebro

Eskilstuna

⊡ **Stockholm**

Tallinn

Pskov · 7

Skagerrak

Trollhättan

Motala

Norrköping

Saaremaa

30°

Göteborg

Borås

Linköping

*Lake
Vättern*

Visby

Fredrikshavn

Fyn

Ålborg

Jönköping

Gotland

Riga

Holstebro

Randers

Halmstad

Växjö

Öland

Liepája

U S S R

Jutland

Århus

Daugavpils

Esbjerg

Kolding

Helsingör

Hälsingborg

Kalmar

Karlskrona

Siauliai

DENMARK

Roskilde

⊡ **Copenhagen**

Klaipeda

Odense

Malmö

Zealand

Slagelse

Bornholm

B A L T I C   S E A

Kaunas

Vilnius

Flensberg

Kaliningrad

Kiel

Gdynia

Stralsund

Oder

Gdańsk

Minsk ■ · 8

Rostock

G E R M A N Y

P O L A N D

10° · 15° · 20° · 25°

89

DENMARK

A B C D E

miles
0   50   100
0 50 100 150
kilometers

54°

NORTH SEA

Flensburg

Kiel

Neumünster

Stralsund
Rostock
Greifs

East Frisian Is.

West Frisian Is.

Wadden Sea

Groningen

Assen

NETHERLANDS

Haarlem

Amsterdam
Apeldoorn
Utrecht

Zwolle

Enschede

52°

Rotterdam
Dordrecht

Arnhem

Maas

Münster

Lübeck

Wismar
Schwerin

Neubranden

Hamburg

Wilhelmshaven

Bremerhaven

Oldenburg

Bremen

Ems

Osnabrück

Weser

Wittenberge

GERMAN

Hannover

Wolfsburg

Potsdam

Brunswick

Bielefeld

Salzgitter

Magdeburg

HARZ MTS

Elbe

Dessau

Eindhoven

Antwerp

Brussels

Maastricht

BELGIUM

Aachen

Liege

Charleroi

Duisburg

Gelsenkirchen

Dortmund

Essen

Bochum

Mönchen-
Gladbach

Wuppertal

Düsseldorf

Cologne

Bonn

Siegen

Kassel

Halle

Weimar

Leipzig

Meisser

Erfurt

Gera

Karl Marx Stadt

Dres

Zwickau

Thuringian
Forest

ARDENNES

EIFEL

Rhine

Wetzlar

Fulda

50°

Koblenz

Mosel

ORE MT

Karlovy V

Charleville-
Mézières

LUXEMBOURG

Luxembourg

Wiesbaden

Frankfurt

Offenbach

Mainz

Darmstadt

Bayreuth

Main

Bamberg

Plzeň

Bohemian
Forest

Thionville

Verdun

Kaiserslautern

Metz

Meuse

Saarbrücken

St. Dizier

Nancy

Mannheim

Heidelberg

Würzburg

Fürth

Nuremberg

Karlsruhe

Strasbourg

Rhine

VOSGES

Offenburg

Stuttgart

Regensburg

Danube

Im

48°

FRANCE

Freiburg

Black Forest

Ulm

Augsburg

Memmingen

Munich

Mulhouse

Lake
Constance

Kempten

Sal

Dijon

Doubs

Besançon

Basel

Winterthur

Zürich

Luzern

Lake
Zürich

LIECHTENSTEIN

Vaduz

Zugspitze 9721'/(2963m)

Innsbruck

AU

Grossglockner
12,460'
(3798m)

JURA MTS

L. de
Neuchâtel

Berne

SWITZERLAND

Chur

ALPS

Lausanne

Merano

Lake
Geneva

Jungfrau
13,653"/(4158m)

ITALY

Bolzano

Geneva

Saône

Saône

6°   8°   10°   12°

F G H J K

BALTIC SEA 1

Gulf of
Gdańsk

Kaliningrad **U S S R**

Chernyakhovsk Kaunas

• Gdynia

Gdańsk

Kołobrzeg • Koszalin • Elbląg Grodno •

Malbork

• Wolin Olsztyn • 2

Szczecin Chojnice •

• Stargard Łomża • Białystok

Piła • Toruń •
• **Bydgoszcz** • Pułtusk

Inowrocław • Włocławek •

Kostrzyn
Brest
Poznań • **P O L A N D** □ **Warsaw** • Siedlce •

Oder

Gubin • Leszno • Kalisz • **Łódź**

Glogów • • Radom **Lublin**

Neisse Görlitz • Legnica • **Wrocław** Zamość • 3

Walbrzych •

Liberec • *SUDETES* Częstochowa •

nad Labem Chorzów • Zabrze • **Katowice** Rzeszów •

□ **Prague** *MTS* Krakow • Tarnow •

Przemyśl •

CZECHOSLOVAKIA **Ostrava** *C A R P A T H I A N*

• Olomouc

• Jihlava *Rysy* 8212'(2499m) *M T S* 4

Gerlachovka Stit Košice •
Brno 8737' Uzhgorod •
(2655m)

Znojmo • *Váh* Mukachevo •

• Gmünd

Krems • Miskolc

Linz □ **Vienna** **Bratislava**

St. Polten *Kékes* 3330'
(1015m) *Tisza* Satu
Mare

Lake
Neusiedler Debrecen

Győr • *Danube* □ **Budapest**

Leoben •
Szombathely • **H U N G A R Y** Oradea • 5

Lake
Graz *Balaton*

RIA Kecskemet •

ROMANIA

• Maribor Szeged • Arad •

Nagykanizsa •

16° 20° 22°

Pécs •

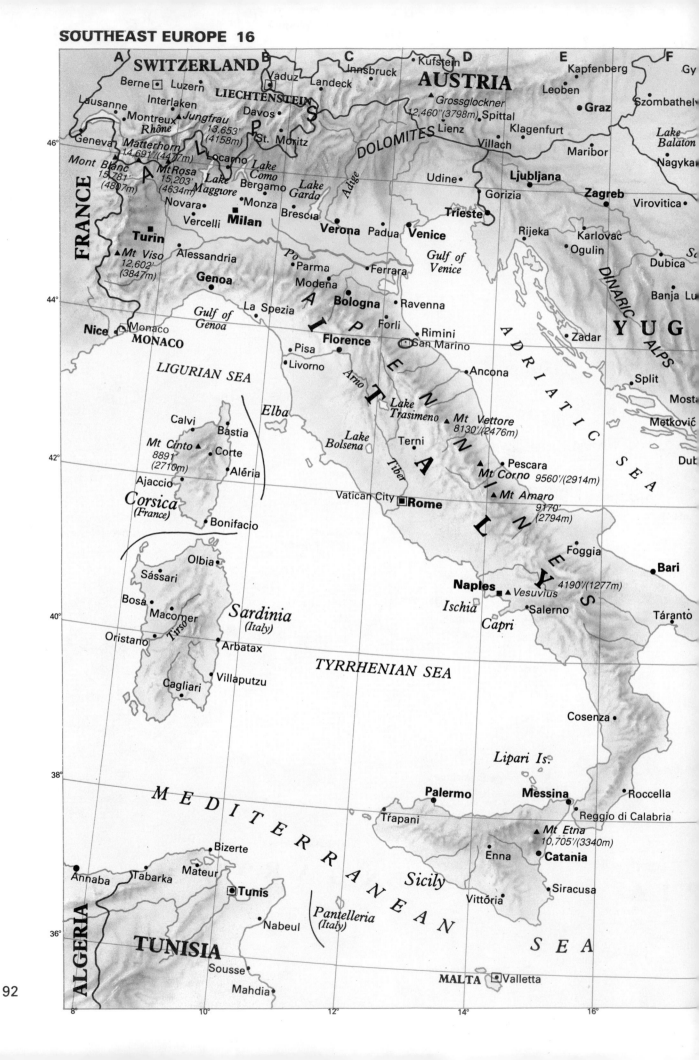

SWITZERLAND

Berne ⊡ Luzern
Lausanne Interlaken
Montreux Jungfrau
Rhône 13,653'
(4158m)
Geneva Matterhorn
14,691'(4477m)
Mont Blanc Mt Rosa
15,781' 15,203'
(4807m) (4634m)

Vaduz
LIECHTENSTEIN
Davos
St. Moritz
Locarno

Lake
Como
Lake
Maggiore
Lake
Bergamo
Garda

Kufstein
Innsbruck
Landeck

AUSTRIA
Grossglockner
12,460"(3798m) Spittal
Lienz
Villach

Kapfenberg
Leoben
Graz Szombathe

Klagenfurt
Maribor
Nagyka
Lake
Balaton

DOLOMITES

Adige

Udine
Gorizia

Ljubljana

Zagreb

Virovitica

FRANCE

Turin

Mt Viso
12,602'
(3847m)

Novara
Vercelli
Milan
Monza
Brescia
Alessandria

Verona
Padua
Venice

Trieste
Rijeka

Karlovac
Ogulin

Dubica

DINARIC

Po
Parma
Modena
Bologna
Ravenna
Forlì

Gulf of
Venice

YUG

Banja Lu

Genoa

La Spezia

Gulf of
Genoa

A
P
P

Florence
Forlì
Rimini
San Marino

ALPS

Nice
Monaco
MONACO

Pisa
Livorno

Arno

Ancona

Zadar

ADRIATIC

Split

LIGURIAN SEA

Elba

E

Lake
Trasimeno
Mt Vettore
8130'(2476m)

Mosta

Metković

Calvi
Bastia

Mt Cinto
8891'
(2710m)
Corte
Aléria

N

Lake
Bolsena

Terni

Tiber

N

Mt Corno
Pescara
9560'(2914m)

SEA

Du

42°

Ajaccio

Corsica
(France)

Bonifacio

Vatican City
Rome

I

Mt Amaro
9170'
(2794m)

N

Olbia
Sássari

N

Foggia
Bari

Bosa
Macomer

Sardinia
(Italy)

Naples
Vesuvius

4190'(1277m)

E

Oristano

Tirso

Arbatax

Ischia
Capri

Salerno

Y

Táranto

Cagliari
Villaputzu

TYRRHENIAN SEA

S

Cosenza

Lipari Is.

Palermo
Messina
Roccella

Trapani

Reggio di Calabria

MEDITERRANEAN

Bizerte

Annaba
Tabarka
Mateur

Tunis

Sicily

Enna

Mt Etna
10,705'(3340m)
Catania

Siracusa

ALGERIA

TUNISIA

Sousse

Nabeul

Pantelleria
(Italy)

Vittòria

SEA

Mahdia

MALTA ⊡ Valletta

46°

44°

40°

38°

36°

8°   10°   12°   14°   16°

A   B   C   D   E   F

G H J K L M N

1

Budapest
Kecskemet
Debrecen
Satu Mare
Oradea
Dej
CARPATHIAN MTS
Botoşani
Iaşi
Kishinev
Tiraspol
Odessa

NGARY
Cluj
Tirgu Mureş
Bacâu

Szeged
Arad
Alba Iulia
Mures

2

Subotica
Timişoara
Lugoj
TRANSYLVANIAN ALPS
Braşov
Galati
Izmail
Sombor
Kikinda
ROMANIA
Negoiu 8361'/(2548m)
Brăila
Tulcea
Zrenjanin

Novi Sad
Belgrade
Turnu Severin
Ploieşti

VIA
Piteşti
Constanţa

3

Kragujevac
Craiova
Bucharest
Danube
Caracal
Giurgiu
Silistra
Mangalia
jevo
Vidin
Ruse
Tolbukhin
Balchik
Lom
Razgrad
Varna
Vratsa
Pleven

Niš
BALKAN MTS
Stara
Zagora
Karnobat
BLACK SEA
Nikšić
Leskovac
BULGARIA
Yambol
Burgas
Titogråd
Pec
Priština
Sofia
Plovdiv
Muritsa

4

Lake
Shkodër
Skopje
Blagoevgrad
BALKAN
PENINSULA
Kirklareli
Midye
Shkodër
Titov Veles
RHODOPE MTS
Smolyan
Edirne
Luleburgaz
nëngjin
Petrich
Komotini
Istanbul
Vardar
Kilkis
Sérrai
Xánthi
Alexandroúpolis
Kesan
Tekirdağ
SEA OF
MARMARA
Tiranë
Ohrid
Lake
Ohrid
Bitola
Edhessa
Thessaloniki
Thásos
Gallipoli
Dardanelles
Bandirma
Bursa
Durrës
Elbasan
Prespa
Lake
Kastoria
Samothráki
Çanakkale
ALBANIA
Korçe
Imroz

5

Vlorë
PINDUS
Mt Olympus
9570'
(2911m)
TURKEY
ASIA MINOR
of Otranto
Ioánnina
Lárisa
Limnos
Ayvalik
Corfu
Igoumenítsa
Trikkala
Vólos
Lésvos
Mitilini
Bergama
Arta
Fársala
Manisa
Préveza
Lamía
Izmir

6

MTS
GREECE
Euboea
Skiros
Khíos
Sámos
Aydin
Mesolóngion
Návpaktos
Khalkis
Marathon
Söke
Pátrai
Ándros
Milâs
Kefallinía
Athens
Tínos
Ikaría
Corinth
Piraeus
Kéa
Argos
Návplion
Kíthnos
Náxos
Marmaris
Zákinthos
Kalámai
Milos
Kos
Rhodes
Pílos
Thíra
Rhodes
Lindos

7

ONIAN
SEA
Kíthira
SEA OF CRETE
Kárpathos
Canea
Crete
Iráklion
Réthimnon

20° 22° 24° 26° 28°

A
B
C
D
E

70°
80°

ARCTIC

Arctic Circle

Franz Josef Land

NORWAY

SWEDEN

DENMARK
Copenhagen

Oslo

Stockholm

FINLAND

BALTIC SEA

Helsinki

Gulf of Finland

Murmansk

BARENTS SEA

Novaya
Zemlya

Sever
Zen

KARA
SEA

Kolguyev

Vaygach

Tay

0°

20°

POLAND
Warsaw

Grodno

LITHUANIA
Kaliningrad

Riga

Tallinn

Novgorod

Pskov

White
Sea

Lake
Onega

Petrozavodsk

Lake Ladoga

Leningrad

Arkhangel'sk

Divna

Syktyvkar

Narodnaya
6214'
(1894m)

Salekhard

West
Siberian
Plain

50°

Lvov

Brest

Chernobyl

Rovno

Vilnius

Minsk

Gomel

Dnepr

Bryansk

Vitebsk

Kalinin

Moscow

Ryazan

Yaroslavl

Cherepovets

Vologda

Kostroma

Kirov

Berezniki

Serov

UNION OF SOVI

Kishinev

Vinnitsa

Dnepropetrovsk

Kiev

Sumy

Orel

Tula

Gorki

Cheboksary

Izhevsk

Perm

Nizhniy Tagil

Zaporozhye

Krivoy
Rog

Kursk

Ul'yanovsk

Kazan

Ufa

Sverdlovsk

Tyumen

Odessa

Kherson

Sea of
Azov

Zhdanov

Kharkov

Voronezh

Tambov

Saratov

Penza

Tol'yatti

Kuybyshev

Orenburg

Chelyabinsk

Kurgan

Omsk

Tomsk

Kem

Simferopol'

Krasnodar

Donetsk

Rostov

Taganrog

Don

Volgograd

Engels

Volga

Ural'sk

Magnitogorsk

Orsk

Kustanay

Petropavlovsk

Novosibirsk

Prokopyevsk

Novokuznetsk

Pavlodar

Barnaul

BLACK
SEA

Stavropol'

Ordzhonikidze

Groznyy

Astrakhan

Ural

Aktyubinsk

Mt. Elbrus 18,480' (5630m)

CAUCASUS MTS

Makhachkala

Guryev

Semipalatinsk

ALT

TURKEY

Batumi

Tbilisi

Yerevan

Mt. Ararat
16,945'
(5165m)

Baku

CASPIAN SEA

ARAL
SEA

Karaganda

Mt. Bel̦uk
15,157
(4506n

40°

40°

Tabriz

ELBURZ MTS

ZAGROS MTS

Tehran

IRAN

Mashhad

Esfahan

Amu Darya

Ashkhabad

Chardzhou

Bukhara

Syr Darya

Chimkent

Tashkent

Leninabad

Samarkand

Osh

Andizhan

Lake
Balkhash

Frunze

Alma-Ata

Hantengri Feng
24,406'
(7439m)

Ur

30°

AFGHANISTAN

Dushanbe

Communism Peak
24,590'
(7495m)

60°

80°

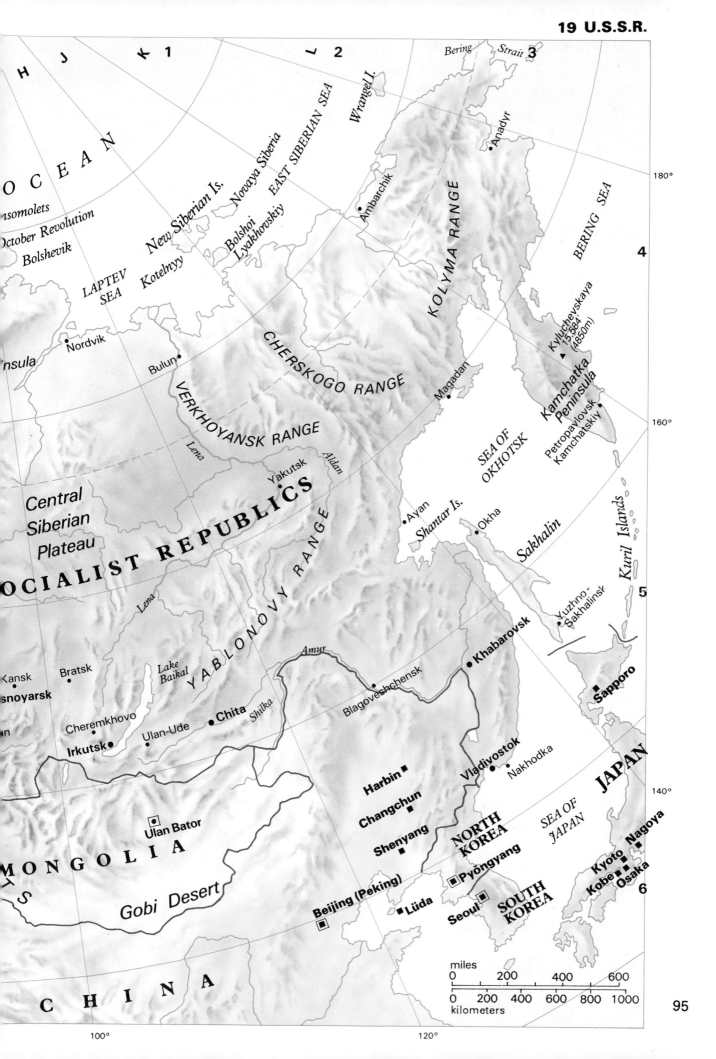

H J K **1** L **2** 3

Bering Strait

4

OCEAN

msomolets

October Revolution

Bolshevik

New Siberian Is.

Novaya Siberia

Bolshoi Lyakhovskiy

EAST SIBERIAN SEA

Wrangel I.

Anadyr

180°

LAPTEV SEA

Kotelnyy

Ambarchik

KOLYMA RANGE

BERING SEA

insula

Nordvik

CHERSKOGO RANGE

Magadan

Kylucheskaya 15,584 (4850m)

Kamchatka Peninsula

160°

VERKHOYANSK RANGE

Bulun

Lena

SEA OF OKHOTSK

Petropavlovsk Kamchatskiy

Central Siberian Plateau

Yakutsk

Aldan

Ayan

Shantar Is.

Okha

Kuril Islands

SOCIALIST REPUBLICS

Lena

YABLONOVY RANGE

Sakhalin

Yuzhno-Sakhalinsk

5

Kansk

Bratsk

Lake Baikal

Amur

Khabarovsk

Sapporo

snoyarsk

Cheremkhovo

Ulan-Ude

Chita

Shilka

Blagoveshchensk

n

Irkutsk

Vladivostok

Nakhodka

JAPAN

Harbin ■

140°

Ulan Bator

Changchun ■

NORTH KOREA

SEA OF JAPAN

Kyoto ■ **Nagoya**

Shenyang ■

Kobe ■ ■

Osaka

MONGOLIA

TS

Gobi Desert

Beijing (Peking)

Lüda

■ **Pyongyang**

Seoul

SOUTH KOREA

6

CHINA

miles
0   200   400   600

0   200 400 600 800 1000
kilometers

100°   120°

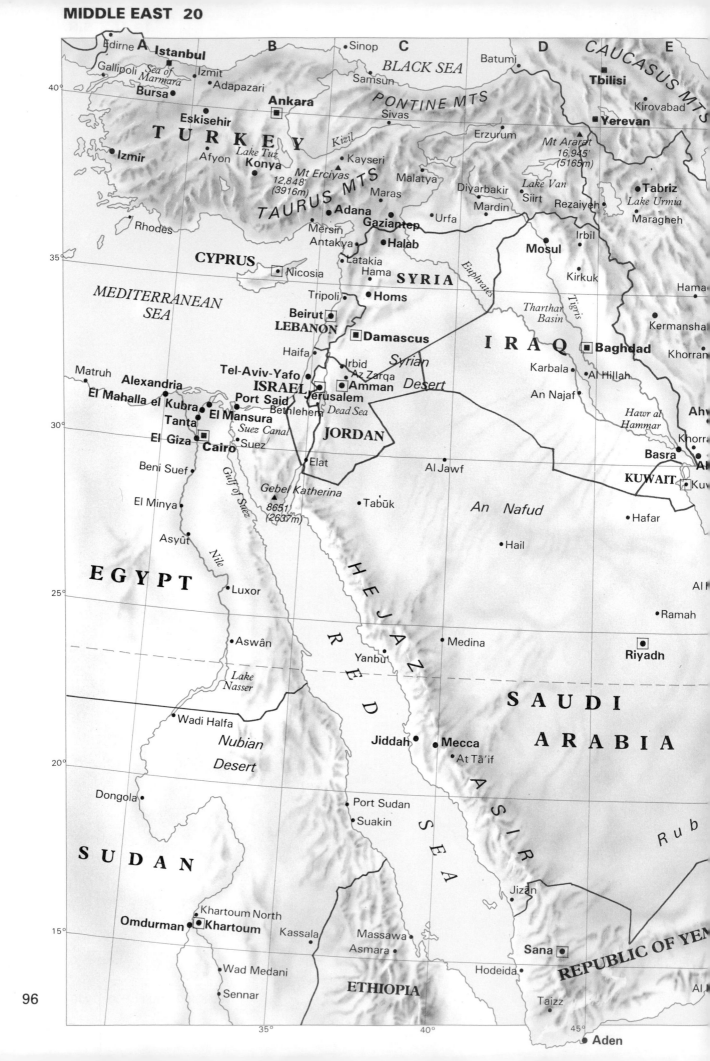

Edirne **A** **Istanbul** **B** • Sinop **C** BLACK SEA • Batumi **D** CAUCASUS **E**
Gallipoli • Izmit Sea of • Samsun • Kirovabad
Bursa Marmara • Adapazari PONTINE MTS **Tbilisi**
40° **Ankara** • Sivas Erzurum Mt Ararat
Eskisehir 16,945' **Yerevan**
Kizil (5165m)
Izmir *Lake Tuz* • Kayseri • Malatya • Diyarbakir *Lake Van* **Tabriz**
Afyon **Konya** Mt Erciyas Maras • Mardin • Siirt • Rezaiyeh *Lake Urmia*
12,848' TAURUS MTS Urfa Irbil • Maragheh
Rhodes (3916m) **Adana** • **Gaziantep** • Mosul • Kirkuk Hama
Mersin **Halab** *Euphrates*
35° CYPRUS Antakya • Latakia IRAQ **Baghdad** Khorran
MEDITERRANEAN • Nicosia Hama *Tharthar* Kermansha
SEA Tripoli **Homs** SYRIA *Basin* Karbala • Al Hillah
Beirut An Najaf *Tigris*
LEBANON **Damascus** Hawr al
Haifa Irbid *Syrian* Hammar **Ah**
Tel-Aviv-Yafo Az Zarqa *Desert* Khorran
ISRAEL **Amman** **Basra**
Jerusalem An Najaf **KUWAIT** Kuw
Matruh **Alexandria** Bethlehem *Dead Sea*
El Mahalla el Kubra **Port Said** **JORDAN**
Tanta **El Mansura** *Suez Canal* Elat Al Jawf
30° **El Giza** **Cairo** • Suez An Nafud
Beni Suef *Gulf of Suez* Tabuk • Hafar
El Minya Gebel Katherina
8651' HEJAZ • Hail
Asyût (2637m) Al H
Nile
EGYPT • Luxor • Ramah
25°
• Aswân Medina **Riyadh**
Lake Yanbu
Nasser R **SAUDI**
Omdurman **Jiddah** **Mecca**
• Wadi Halfa E • At Tâ'if **ARABIA**
Nubian D
Desert A
Dongola • S S
SUDAN I
Port Sudan E R
• Suakin A
15° Khartoum North
Omdurman **Khartoum** Kassala • Massawa
• Asmara Sana
• Wad Medani • REPUBLIC OF YEM
• Hodeida Al
ETHIOPIA • Taizz
35° 40° 45° • Aden

96

F   G   H   J   K

1

CASPIAN SEA

U. S. S. R.

Tashkent ■

Samarkand •

Ashkhabad •

KOPET RANGE

Amu Darya

Dushanbe ●

2

Babol • Gorgan

BURZ MTS

▲ Demavend 18,600'
(5604m)

Mashhad ●

Mazar-i-Sharif •

Faizabad •

HINDU KUSH

Gilgit •

75°

Baghlan •

Tirich Mir
25,263
(7690m)

Tehran

Rey •

Dasht-e-Kavir

Herat •

Charikar •

Jalalabad •

Peshawar •

Islamabad
■

m

Shah Fuladi
16,243
(5143m) ▲

Kabul ⊡

Khyber
Pass

Wah •

Rawalpindi ●

3

RAN

Esfahan •

Birjand •

Ghazni •

Gujrat •

Gujranwala ●

Sargodha •

Lahore ■

Yazd •

Farah •

AFGHANISTAN

ZAGROS MTS

Dasht-e-Lut

Helmand

Kandahar •

Faisalabad ●

Kerman •

Quetta •

Multan ●

Bahawalpur •

Shiraz •

Kalat •

SULAIMAN RANGE

Bikaner •

4

shehr

PAKISTAN

Indus

Sukkur •

INDIA

Bandar-e-
Lengeh •

Bandar Abbas •

Jodhpur •

RAIN

ama

Strait of Hormuz

OMAN

Gwadar •

Hyderabad •

Sharjah •

Doha •

TAR

Dubai •

Chah Bahar •

Karachi ■

Abu Dhabi ⊡

Al Khaburah •

Gulf of Oman

Ahmadabad ■

**UNITED
ARAB
EMIRATES**

Muscat
⊡

Tropic of Cancer

5

Jamnagar •

Rajkot ●

ali

OMAN

Salalah •

A R A B I A N   S E A

6

miles

0   100   200   300

0   100 200 300 400 500
kilometers

Qishn •

7

55°   60°   65°   70°

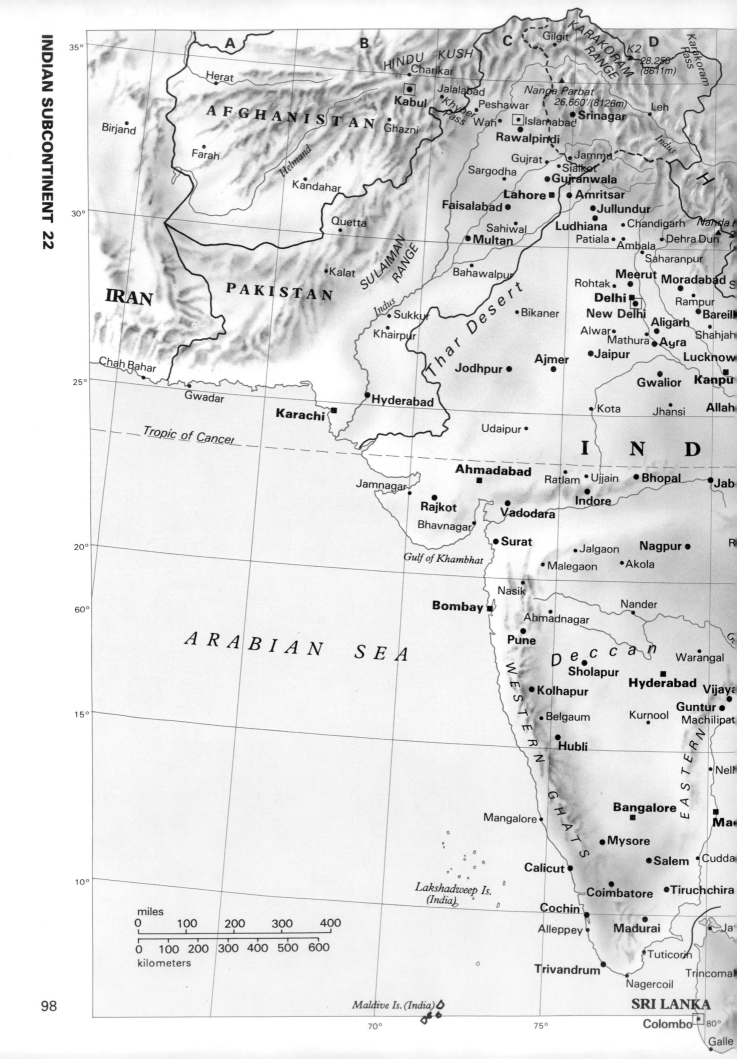

A   B   C   D

35°

HINDU KUSH

KARAKORAM RANGE

Gilgit
K2
28,250′
(8611m)

Karakoram Pass

Herat

Charikar

Jalalabad
Khyber Pass
Peshawar

Nanga Parbat
26,660′/(8126m)

Leh

Kabul
Ghazni

Wah
Islamabad
Srinagar

Birjand

Rawalpindi

Jammu

AFGHANISTAN

Gujrat
Sialkot

H

Farah

Sargodha
Gujranwala

Helmand

Lahore
Amritsar
Jullundur

Kandahar

Faisalabad
Ludhiana
Chandigarh

Nanda

30°

Sahiwal
Patiala
Ambala
Dehra Dun

Multan
Saharanpur

IRAN

Quetta

Bahawalpur

Rohtak
Meerut
Moradabad

PAKISTAN

Delhi
Rampur

S

Kalat

SULAIMAN RANGE

Indus
Sukkur

New Delhi
Aligarh
Bareil

Alwar
Mathura
Agra
Shahjah

Bikaner

Khairpur

Ajmer
Jaipur
Lucknow

25°

Jodhpur

Gwalior
Kanpu

Chah Bahar

Thar Desert

Kota
Jhansi
Allah

Gwadar

Hyderabad

I   N   D

Udaipur

Tropic of Cancer

Karachi

Ahmadabad

Ratlam
Ujjain
Bhopal
Jab

Jamnagar

Rajkot

Vadodara

Indore

Bhavnagar

Surat

Jalgaon
Nagpur

Gulf of Khambhat

Malegaon
Akola

20°

Nasik

Nander

Bombay

Ahmadnagar

Deccan

60°

Pune

Warangal

ARABIAN SEA

Sholapur

Hyderabad
Vijaya

Kolhapur

Guntur
Machilipat

Belgaum
Kurnool

WESTERN GHATS

15°

Hubli

EASTERN GHATS

Bangalore

Nell

Mangalore

Ma

Mysore

GHATS

Calicut

Salem
Cudda

Coimbatore
Tiruchchira

Cochin

Lakshadweep Is.
(India)

Alleppey
Madurai

10°

Tuticorin

Trivandrum

Trincoma

Nagercoil

miles
0   100   200   300   400

0   100   200   300   400   500   600
kilometers

Maldive Is. (India)

SRI LANKA

Colombo

Galle

70°   75°   80°

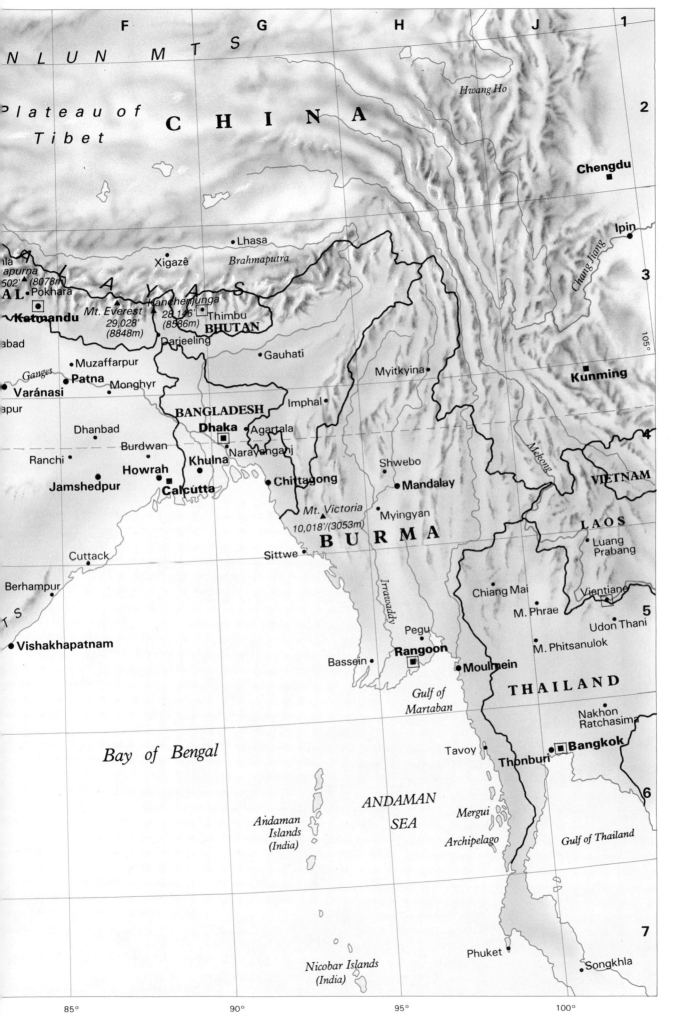

F   G   H   J   1

N L U N M T S

*Plateau of
Tibet* **C H I N A**

2

Hwang Ho

Chengdu ■

Ipin ■

• Lhasa

Xigazê •   *Brahmaputra*

3

apurna
502' ▲ (8078m)
AL •Pokhara   *Kanchenjunga*
Katmandu   ▲ 28,146'
  Mt. Everest   (8586m) □ Thimbu
  29,028'   **BHUTAN**
  (8848m)   Darjeeling•

Chang Jiang

105°

abad

Ganges   • Muzaffarpur   • Gauhati
• **Patna**   Monghyr •
Varánasi

Myitkyina •

Kunming ■

apur

Dhanbad •   **BANGLADESH**   Imphal •
    Burdwan •   **Dhaka** • • Agartala
Ranchi •   □ Narayanganj•
  Howrah   **Khulna**   Shwebo •
Jamshedpur   **Calcutta**   • **Chittagong**
          ■   • **Mandalay**

4

VIETNAM

Mt. Victoria
10,018'/(3053m) ▲   • Myingyan

B U R M A   **L A O S**

Cuttack •   Sittwe •

Berhampur •

Irrawaddy

  Chiang Mai •
     • Luang
      Prabang

Vientiane

T S

• **Vishakhapatnam**

• Pegu

Rangoon
□

Bassein •

  • Moulmein

M. Phrae •
     Udon Thani •

M. Phitsanulok •

5

*Gulf of
Martaban*

T H A I L A N D

Mekong

Nakhon
Ratchasima •

Bay of Bengal

Tavoy •

Thonburi• □ **Bangkok**

6

*ANDAMAN
SEA*

*Andaman
Islands
(India)*

*Mergui

Archipelago*

Gulf of Thailand

7

Phuket •

*Nicobar Islands
(India)*

• Songkhla

85°   90°   95°   100°

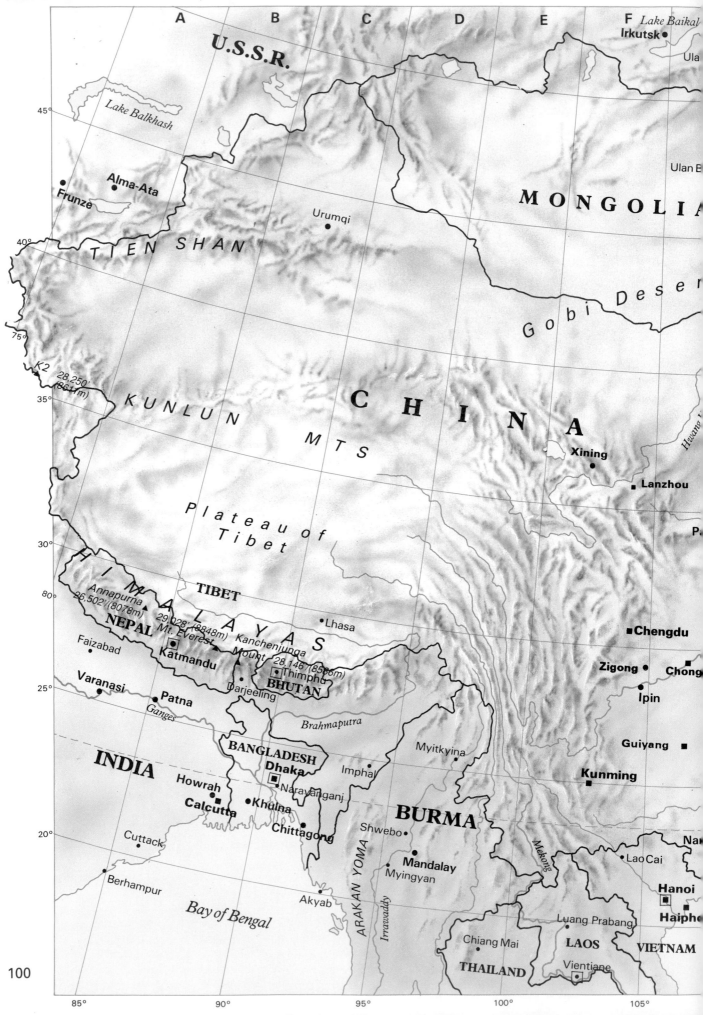

A   B   C   D   E   F

Lake Baikal

Irkutsk

Ula

U.S.S.R.

Lake Balkhash

MONGOLIA

Ulan B

45°

40°

75°

35°

30°

80°

25°

20°

Frunze

Alma-Ata

Urumqi

TIEN SHAN

G o b i   D e s e r

C H I N A

K U N L U N

M T S

K2
28,250
(8611m)

Xining

■ **Lanzhou**

P l a t e a u   o f
Tibet

Hwang

P.

TIBET

H I M
Annapurna
26,502 (8078m) ▲

29,028 (8848m)
Mt. Everest

A L A Y A S

•Lhasa

Chengdu

NEPAL

Faizabad

⊡
Katmandu

Mount
Kanchenjunga
28,146 (8586m) ▲

⊡
Thimphu

BHUTAN

Zigong •

Chong

• **Ipin**

Varanasi

Patna
•

Darjeeling

Ganges

Brahmaputra

Guiyang ■

INDIA

BANGLADESH

Dhaka
⊡
•Narayanganj

Myitkyina

Kunming

Howrah
■
Calcutta

• **Khulna**

Chittagong

Imphal

BURMA

Na

Cuttack

Shwebo
•

Mandalay
•

Myingyan

Mekong

• Lao Cai

Berhampur

ARAKAN YOMA

Akyab

Irrawaddy

Bay of Bengal

Hanoi
⊡

Haiphe

Luang Prabang

Chiang Mai

LAOS

VIETNAM

THAILAND

Vientiane
⊡

85°   90°   95°   100°   105°

H   J   K   L   M   N   O

Amur

Blagoveshchensk

U.S.S.R.

Sakhalin

Khabarovsk

Yuzhno-
Sakhalinsk

■ Qiqihar   • Jiamusi

Hokkaido

Asahikawa

Harbin ■   Mudanjiang

Sapporo   ■

Hakodate

■ **Jilin**

Changchun •   Vladivostok

Aomori

Liaoyuan •

Nakhodka

• Chongjin

DEMOCRATIC PEOPLE'S

Akita

Honshu

Sendai

Fuxin •   **Fushun**   Tonghua •

REPUBLIC OF KOREA

SEA OF JAPAN

Niigata

Shenyang •■   • Benxi

Iwaki

JAPAN

Hohhot   **Zhangjiakou**   Jinzhou •   Anshan •

Hungnam •

•   Datong

Antung •

□ *Pyongyang*

Kanazawa •

Tokyo

Kawasaki

ou

Beijing (Peking) □   ■ **Tangshan**

Lüda ■

□ Seoul

Fuji

Chiba

Nagoya 12,388 (3776m)▲ **Yokohama**

Baoding •   **Tianjin** ■

REPUBLIC

Inchon •

Kyoto ■   Shizuoka

OF KOREA

Taejon •

Kobe ■ ● **Osaka**

Taiyuan ■   ■ **Shijiazhuang**

Chonju •   ■ **Taegu**

Hiroshima •   Okayama •   Wakayama •

Weifang •

Pusan ■

Jinan •   Po-Shan •

Kwangju •   Masan •

Matsuyama •

Zhengzhou ■   **Qingdao** ■

*YELLOW
SEA*

Kitakyushu ■

Shikoku

Luoyang •   • Kaifeng

Fukuoka ■

Kumamoto •

Xuzhou ■

Nagasaki •   Miyazaki •

Bengbu •

Kagoshima •   *Kyushu*

Huainan •   Zhenjiang •

Hefei •   **Nanjing** ■   • Wuxi

EAST

Wuhu •   **Suzhou** ■ ■ **Shanghai**

CHINA

Huanggang • ■ **Wuhan**

Hangzhou •

SEA

Chang Jiang)

Ningbo •

Changsha •   Nanchang •

• Wenzhou

Xiangtan • •• **Zhuzhou**

Naha •

PACIFIC

aoyang •

Ryukyu Is.

Hengyang •

Fuzhou •

OCEAN

Taipei
□

Tropic of Cancer

uzhou

Amoy •   • T'aichung

**Guangzhou
(Canton)** •

T'ainan •   **TAIWAN**

Wuzhou •   • Shantou

Xi Jiang

Kowloon •   **Kaohsiung** ■

Macao
(Portugal)   **Hong Kong**
(British)

SOUTH

Haikou •

CHINA SEA

Hainan

PHILIPPINES

miles
0   200   400

0   200   400   600
kilometers

1

2

3

4

5

6

7

145°

140°

135°

115°   120°   125°   130°

SOUTHEAST ASIA 26

A • Shwebo
• **Mandalay**
Myingyan

B R. Red
• Lao Cai
Nanning
CHINA
Guangzhou (Canton)
Shantou E
T'aina
C
Kaohsi

BURMA
R. Irrawaddy
Salween
• Pegu
• **Rangoon**
Moulmein

Chiang Mai
Luang Prabang
• Vientiane
THAILAND
Udon Thani
Nakhon Sawan
Nakhon Ratchasima

VIETNAM
• Vinh
• Hanoi
Haiphong

Macao
(Portugal)
Kowloon
Hong Kong
(Britain)

Haikou
Hainan

• Hué
• **Da Nang**

LAOS
ANNAM HIGHLANDS
R. Mekong

Ubon Ratchathani
Pakse
Attopeu

• Qui Nhon

Tavoy
Bangkok
• Sisophon
Battambang
KAMPUCHEA
• Kratie
Tonle Sap
Phnom Penh

Kampot
My Tho
Ho Chi Min City
Rach Gia
Can Tho

• Nha Trang
• Cam Ranh

SOUTH CHINA
SEA

Palawan

SU
SI

Gulf of Thailand

Phuket
• Trang
• Songkhla
• Kota Baharu

Banda Aceh
George Town

MALAYSIA

Kudat
Kota Kinabalu
Bandar Seri Begawan
BRUNEI
Sabah
• Tawau

Ipoh
Medan
Pematangsiantar
Simeulue
Lake Toba
Kuala Lumpur
• Gemas
Johor Baharu
Singapore

Strait of Malacca

Nias

Kuching
• Sibu
Sarawak
Murud
7999'
(2439m)

Pakanbaru

Pontianak
Sintang

• Samarinda

Siberut
Padang
Jambi
Kerinci
12,467'
(3805m)
Bangka
BARISAN RANGE
Sumatra
Palembang
Belitung

Borneo
• Balikpapan

Banjarmasin

Makassar Strait

Majene
Rantekomb
11,335'/(345
Watampo

Ujung Pandang

Tanjungkarang-Telukbetung

JAVA SEA

I N D O N

FLORE
Lesser Su

Jakarta
Bogor
Semarang
Surakarta
Kediri
Surabaya
Bandung
Yogyakarta
Malang
Java
Lombok
Raba

INDIAN OCEAN

Bali
Sumbawa
Wainga
Sum

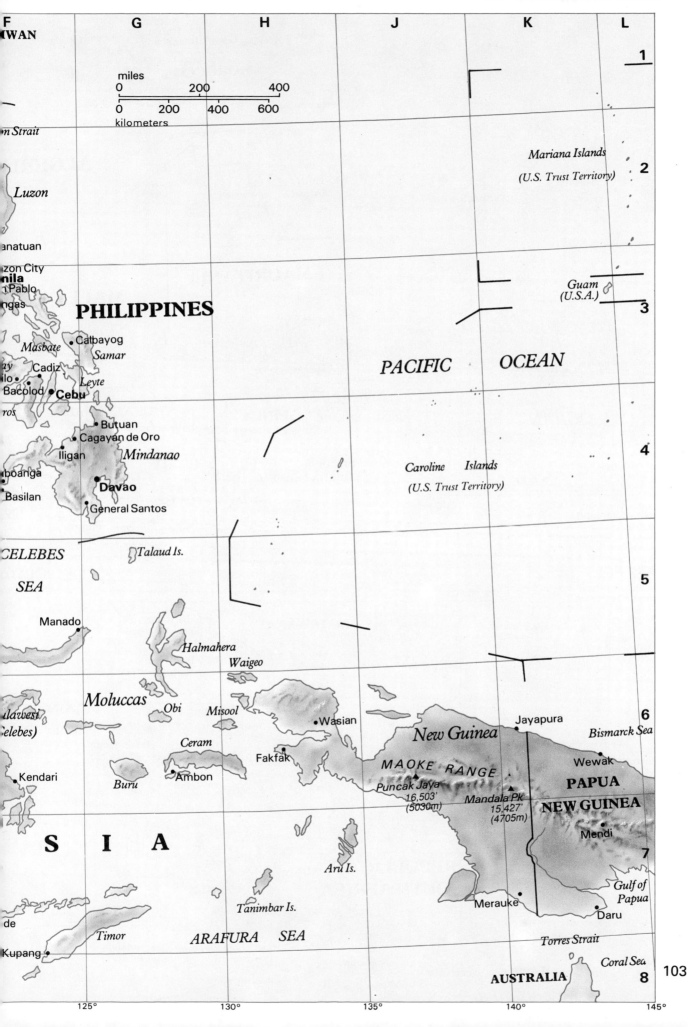

F   **G**   **H**   **J**   **K**   **L**

WAN

miles
0   200   400

0   200   400   600
kilometers

Mariana Islands
(*U.S. Trust Territory*)

n Strait

Luzon

anatuan

zon City
nila
Pablo
ngas

PHILIPPINES

Guam
(*U.S.A.*)

PACIFIC   *OCEAN*

•Calbayog
Masbate   *Samar*
y   Cadiz
lo   *Leyte*
Bacolod   **Cebu**
ros

•Butuan
•Cagayan de Oro
Iligan   *Mindanao*
boanga
•**Davao**
•Basilan
•General Santos

Caroline   *Islands*
(*U.S. Trust Territory*)

CELEBES

SEA

•*Talaud Is.*

Manado•

Moluccas   *Obi*
lawesi   *Misool*
elebes)

Halmahera
Waigeo

•Wasian

New Guinea

Jayapura•

Bismarck Sea

•Kendari
Ceram
Fakfak•
Buru   Ambon•

MAOKE RANGE

Puncak Jaya▲
16,503'
(5030m)

Mandala Pk▲
15,427'
(4705m)

•Wewak

PAPUA
NEW GUINEA

•Mendi

S   I   A

Aru Is.

*Gulf of
Papua*

de
Kupang

Tanimbar Is.

Timor   *ARAFURA*   *SEA*

•Merauke

Torres Strait

•Daru

Coral Sea

AUSTRALIA

1   2   3   4   5   6   7   8

125°   130°   135°   140°   145°

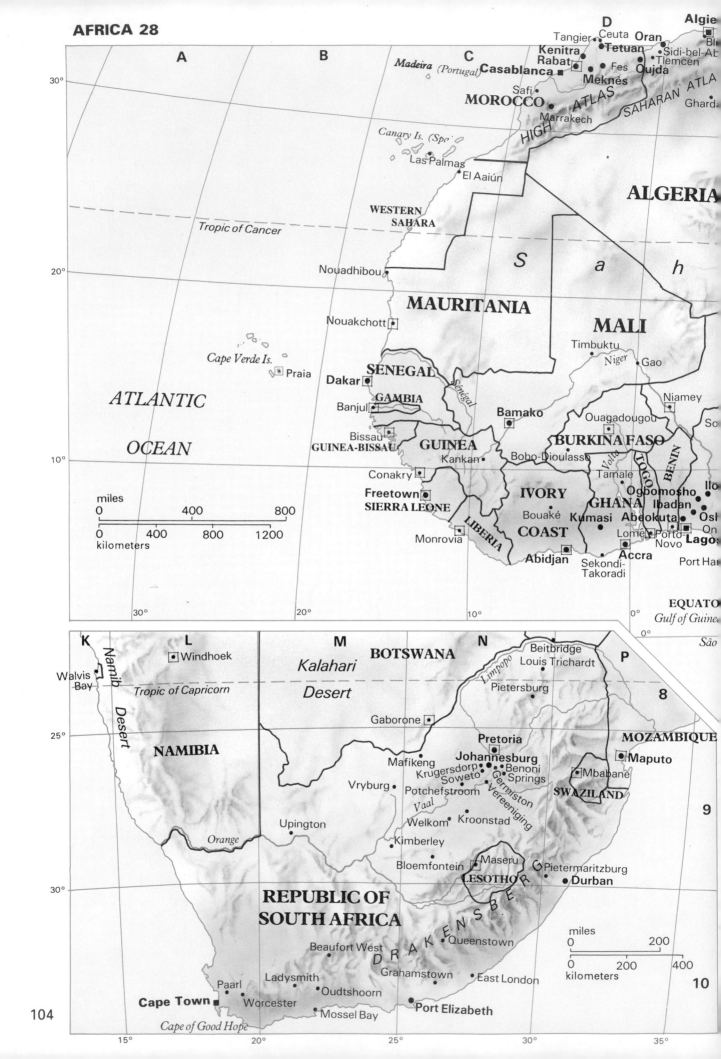

ATLANTIC

OCEAN

Tropic of Cancer

MAURITANIA

MALI

WESTERN
SAHARA

ALGERIA

Sahel

Nouadhibou

Timbuktu
Niger • Gao

Nouakchott

Cape Verde Is.

Praia

SENEGAL
Dakar

Niamey

GAMBIA
Banjul

Bamako

Ouagadougou

Senegal

Bissau
GUINEA-BISSAU

GUINEA
Kankan •

Bobo-Dioulasso

BURKINA FASO

BENIN

TOGO

Conakry

Tamale

Volta

Ogbomosho   Ilo

miles
0   400   800

Freetown
SIERRA LEONE

IVORY

GHANA   Ibadan

Bouaké •   Kumasi

Abeokuta

Osh

0   400   800   1200
kilometers

LIBERIA

COAST

Lomé   Porto-

On

Monrovia

Novo   **Lago**

Abidjan

Sekondi-   **Accra**

Port Ha

Takoradi

EQUATO

Gulf of Guine

São

Tangier • Ceuta   **Oran**   **Algie**

D

Kenitra   **Tetuan**   Bl

Rabat   Sidi-bel-Ab

Casablanca   Fes   Tlemcen

Madeira   (Portugal)   **Oujda**

Meknès

MOROCCO   Safi   ATLA

Marrakech   HIGH ATLAS   SAHARAN ATLA

Ghard

Canary Is. (Spa

Las Palmas

El Aaiún

K   *Namib*   **L**

M   **N**

Beitbridge

P

Walvis   • Windhoek

BOTSWANA

Louis Trichardt

Bay

Tropic of Capricorn

Kalahari

Limpopo

Pietersburg

8

Desert

Desert

Gaborone

MOZAMBIQUE

NAMIBIA

Pretoria

Mafikeng

Johannesburg

Maputo

Krugersdorp   Benoni

Vryburg

Soweto   Springs

Mbabane

Potchefstroom

Germiston

9

Vaal

Vereeniging

SWAZILAND

Upington

Welkom   Kroonstad

Orange

Kimberley

Bloemfontein   Maseru   Pietermaritzburg

LESOTHO   • Durban

REPUBLIC OF

SOUTH AFRICA

Queenstown

miles

0   200

Beaufort West

D

Grahamstown

R

0   200   400

kilometers

Ladysmith   • East London

10

Paarl

Oudtshoorn

Cape Town   Worcester

Mossel Bay   **Port Elizabeth**

Cape of Good Hope

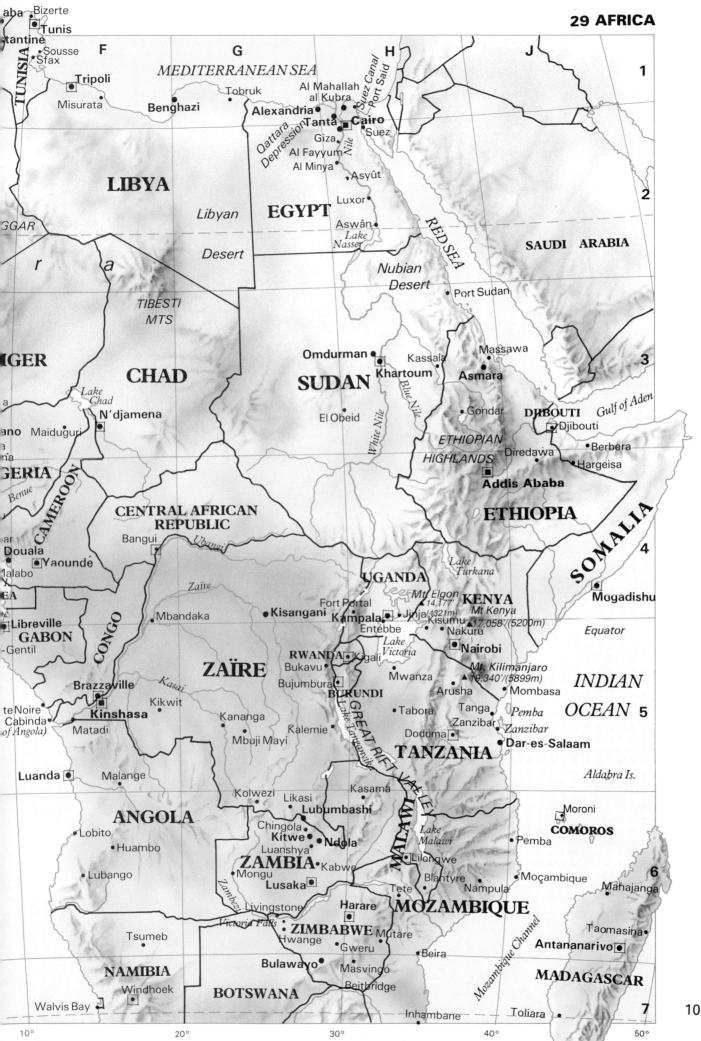

aba • Bizerte
□ **Tunis**
antine •
• Sousse
• Sfax

F

G

MEDITERRANEAN SEA

H

J

1

□ **Tripoli**
• Misurata

TUNISIA

LIBYA

• Tobruk

• Benghazi

Al Mahallah
al Kubra
Alexandria •
Tanta •
Qattara Depression
• Giza
• Al Fayyum
• Al Minya

Suez Canal
Port Said
□ **Cairo**
• Suez

2

Libyan

EGYPT

Nile

• Asyût

• Luxor

RED SEA

SAUDI ARABIA

IGGAR

r   *a*

Desert

• Aswân
Lake Nasser

Nubian Desert

• Port Sudan

TIBESTI MTS

CHAD

Lake Chad

□ **N'djamena**

ano • Maiduguri

SUDAN

• Omdurman
□ **Khartoum**

• El Obeid

White Nile

• Kassala

• Massawa

• **Asmara**

• Gondar

ETHIOPIAN HIGHLANDS

DJIBOUTI
□ **Djibouti**

Gulf of Aden

• Berbera

• Hargeisa

3

a

GERIA

CAMEROON

ar •
• **Douala**
□ **Yaounde**

Malabo
X

CENTRAL AFRICAN REPUBLIC

• Bangui

Ubangi

• Diredawa

□ **Addis Ababa**

ETHIOPIA

SOMALIA

4

é •

GABON

CONGO

□ **Mogadishu**

Libreville •
-Gentil •

Zaïre

ZAÏRE

• Mbandaka

• **Kisangani**

UGANDA

Mt Elgon 14,177'

Fort Portal •
Kampala □ • Jinja *(1321m)*
• Entebbe
Lake Victoria
• Kisumu

KENYA

Mt Kenya ▲17,058'(5200m)
• Nakuru

Equator

Kasai

Brazzaville •

RWANDA □ Kigali
• Bukavu
• Bujumbura
BURUNDI

□ **Nairobi**

Mt. Kilimanjaro ▲19,340'(5899m)

INDIAN

te Noire •
Cabinda (of Angola)

□ **Kinshasa**
• Matadi

• Kikwit

ZAÏRE

• Kananga

• Mbuji Mayi

• Mwanza

• Arusha

• Tabora
GREAT RIFT VALLEY

• Mombasa

• Tanga
• Zanzibar
Zanzibar
• **Dar-es-Salaam**

OCEAN 5

Luanda □

• Malange

• Kolwezi

• Likasi

Lake Tanganyika

□ Dodoma

TANZANIA

Aldabra Is.

ANGOLA

• Lobito

• Huambo

• Lubango

Kitwe •
• Chingola
• Luanshya
ZAMBIA
• Mongu

Lubumbashi

• **Ndola**

• Kabwe

• Kasama

Lake Malawi
MALAWI
• Lilongwe
M

• Pemba

Moroni
□
COMOROS

• Mahajanga

6

• Tsumeb

NAMIBIA

• Windhoek
□

Lusaka □

Zambezi
• Livingstone
Victoria Falls

BOTSWANA

• Mongu

• Harare •
ZIMBABWE
• Mutare
• Hwange
• Gweru
• Bulawayo
• Masvingo
• Beitbridge

Tete •

MOZAMBIQUE

• Blantyre

• Nampula

• Beira

• Moçambique

Mozambique Channel

• Taomasina

Antananarivo □

MADAGASCAR

• Toliara

7

• Inhambane

□ Walvis Bay

10°   20°   30°   40°   50°

ALASKA RANGE
Mt. McKinley
20,320'
(6198m)
Yukon
Fairbanks
ALASKA (U.S.A.)
Anchorage
Seward
Gulf of Alaska
Mt. Logan
19,524'
(5951m)
Mt. St. Elias
18,009'(5489m)
ST. ELIAS MTS
PACIFIC
OCEAN
140°
Queen
Charlotte Is.
Dawson
YUKON
MACKENZIE MTS
Whitehorse
Skagway
Juneau
COASTAL MTS
ROCKY
Mackenzie
BEAUFORT
SEA
Banks I.
Amundsen
Gulf
Coppermine
Great Bear
Lake
Bathurst Inlet
McClure Strait
Melville I.
Viscount Mel
Sound
Prince
Wales
McClintock
Channel
Victoria
Island
NORTHWEST TERRITORIES
Yellowknife
Fort Reliance
Great
Slave Lake
Eskimo P
C
A
N
Prince George
BRITISH
COLUMBIA
SELKIRK MTS
Vancouver I.
Victoria
Vancouver
Olympia Tacoma
Seattle
WASHINGTON
Spokane
Mt. St. Helens 8362
8364
(2549m)
Snake
OREGON
Portland
Salem
CALIFORNIA
Sacramento Reno
Oakland Carson City
San Francisco NEVADA
Fort St. John
M
O
U
N
T
A
I
N
S
UNITED
STATES
Boise
IDAHO
OF
Great Falls
Helena
MONTANA
Billings
WYOMING
Ogden
Salt Lake City
Provo
UTAH
ALBERTA
Edmonton
Jasper
Banff
Calgary
Lethbridge
SASKATCHEWAN
Saskatchewan
Saskatoon
Moose Jaw
Regina
Brandon
NORTH DAKOTA
Bismarck
South DAKOTA
Pierre
Cheyenne
COLORADO
NEBRASKA
MANITOB
Lake
Winnipeg
Winnipeg
Ke
Church
MINNES
Minneapo
St.
Fargo
Sioux Falls
AMERICA
Missouri
Sioux C
IO

65°
150°
60°
55°
50°
45°
40°
130°
120°
110°
100°
70°

Devon I.

Lancaster Sound

Baffin Bay

GREENLAND
(Denmark)

• Angmagssalik

Baffin
Island

Foxe
Basin

Prince
Charles I.

Davis Strait

Godthåb •

Julianehaab •

Southampton I.

Hudson Strait

sterfield Inlet

A   **D**   **A**

Hudson Bay

ATLANTIC

OCEAN

Nain •

Labrador Peninsula

Battle Harbour •

NEWFOUNDLAND

LABRADOR

QUEBEC

Newfoundland

St. John's ★

Corner Brook •

ONTARIO

St. Lawrence

Gulf of
St. Lawrence

St. Pierre &
Miquelon
(French)

• Fort Rupert

NEW
BRUNSWICK

PRINCE EDWARD I.
Charlottetown ★

Sydney •

Chicoutimi •

Quebec ★

Fredericton ★

Moncton •

NOVA SCOTIA

Thunder Bay ★

Timmins •

Trois-Riviéres

MAINE

Saint John •

Halifax ★

Montreal ■

Bangor •

Augusta ★

Lake Superior

Sudbury •

Hull

Sault Sainte Marie

North Bay •

Ottawa ●

Burlington

MICHIGAN

Peterborough •

Kingston

VERMONT

Concord ★

Lake Huron

Montpelier ★

NEW
HAMPSHIRE

WISCONSIN

Toronto ★

Lake
Ontario

Syracuse •

Boston ★

Green Bay •

Kitchener •

Hamilton ●

Albany •

MASS.

Providence ★

Milwaukee ★

Grand Rapids •

Niagara

NEW YORK

Hartford ★

CONN. R.I.

Madison •

Lansing ★

London •

Brantford

Lake Michigan

Windsor •

Detroit ●

Lake Erie

Newark ■

New York ■

Chicago ■

Cleveland •

PENNSYLVANIA

Philadelphia ■

N.J.

ILLINOIS   INDIANA   Toledo •   OHIO

miles
0   200   400

0   200   400   600
kilometers

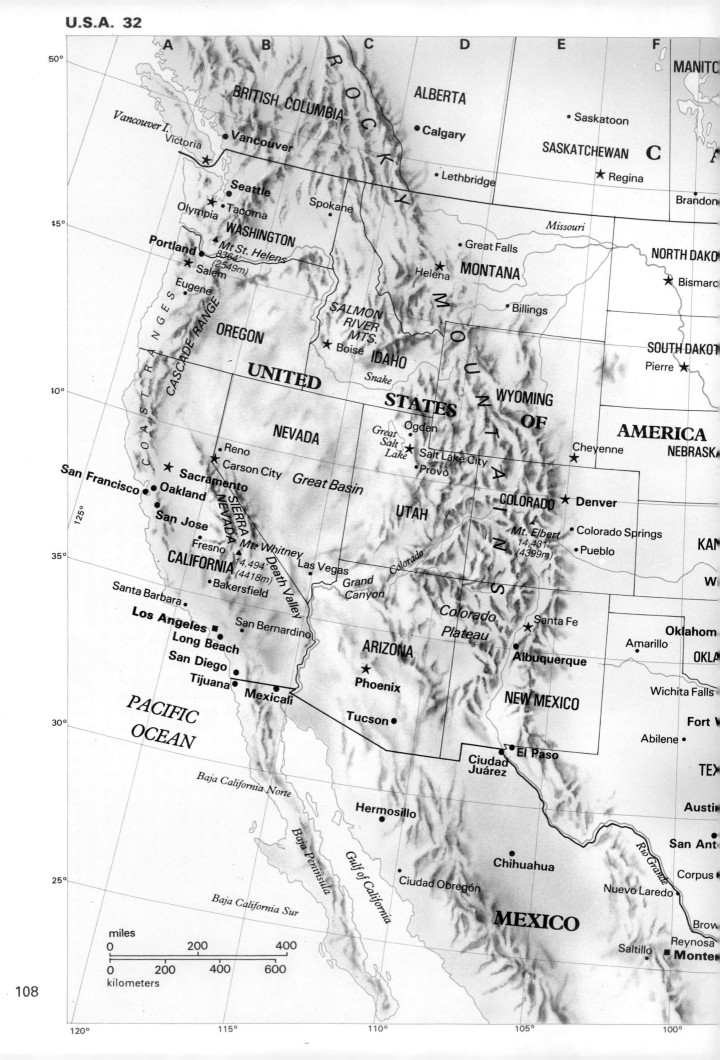

Fort Rupert •

A D A

ONTARIO

QUEBEC

St. Lawrence

NEW BRUNSWICK

peg •

Thunder Bay • Timmins • Quebec ★

Trois-Riviéres •

Fredericton ★

Saint John •

Lake Superior Montreal ■ MAINE

Bangor •

MINNESOTA Saulte Sainte Marie Ottawa ■ Montpelier Augusta ★

Portland •

Minneapolis • MICHIGAN Peterborough • Kingston NEW YORK NEW HAMPSHIRE Concord ★

Falls • • St. Paul WISCONSIN *Lake Huron* Toronto ★ *Lake Ontario* Utica • Albany • Worcester • Boston

Green Bay • Hamilton ★ Rochester • Syracuse • Hartford ★ MASS.

ux City IOWA Madison • Grand Rapids • *Lake Michigan Niagara Falls* Buffalo ★ *Hudson* CONN. R.I. Providence

Cedar Rapids • Milwaukee ★ Lansing ★ London • *Lake Erie* Cleveland • PENNSYLVANIA Newark ★ New York ■

Des Moines ★ Davenport • Detroit ■ Toledo ★ Youngstown • Pittsburgh ★ MTS. Trenton • Jersey City

Omaha Chicago ■ Peoria • Akron • Harrisburg • Philadelphia ■

INDIANA OHIO Dayton • Columbus ★ Dover ■ NEW JERSEY

ILLINOIS Decatur • Cincinnati ● Baltimore ■ DEL.

Kansas City Springfield • Indianapolis ★ Charleston • Washington MARYLAND

Jefferson City • WEST VIRGINIA Washington D.C. Annapolis ★

eka • ★ St. Louis Evansville • Louisville ★ VIRGINIA

MISSOURI *Ohio* Frankfort ★ Richmond • Norfolk ●

Springfield • KENTUCKY APPALACHIAN

sa *OZARK PLATEAU* Winston- Greensboro •

Salem Raleigh ★

★ Nashville ▲ Mt. Mitchell NORTH CAROLINA

Fort Smith • *Tennessee* Knoxville • 6684' Charlotte ●

ansas TENNESSEE (2037m)

Memphis ● Chattanooga • SOUTH CAROLINA

Little Rock ★ Huntsville • Columbia ★

ARKANSAS Augusta • Charleston •

Birmingham ● ★ Atlanta

Monroe • Tuscaloosa • ALABAMA Columbus • Savannah •

Shreveport • MISSISSIPPI Montgomery ★ GEORGIA

Jackson ★ GEORGIA

Mobile • Jacksonville ●

LOUISIANA Baton Rouge ★ Pensacola • Tallahassee ★

ston ■ Port Arthur • New Orleans ● FLORIDA

• Galveston Orlando • *Cape Canaveral*

Tampa ●

Gulf of Mexico Fort Lauderdale •

The Everglades Miami ● Nassau ■

BAHAMAS

See page 118 for Alaska and page 116 for Hawaii

Florida Keys

CUBA

ATLANTIC OCEAN

70°

95°   90°   85°   80°   75°

A   B   C   D   E   F

San Diego
Tijuana
Mexicali
★ Phoenix
ARIZONA
Tucson

Albuquerque
NEW MEXICO
Amarillo

MISSOURI
Tulsa
Fort Smith
★ Oklahoma City
OKLAHOMA
Little Rock
ARKANSAS
Mem
Tusca
Arkansas
Mississippi

UNITED STATES OF AMERICA

Ciudad
Juárez
El Paso
Fort Worth ● ● Dallas
TEXAS
Red
Shreveport
MISSISSIPPI
★ Jackson
Mobil
LOUISIANA
Baton Rouge
New Orle

Hermosillo
SIERRA
Chihuahua
Rio Grande
San Antonio
Houston
Galveston
★ Austin

Ciudad
Obregón
Nuevo Laredo
Corpus Christi
Gulf of Mexico

Baja California Norte
Baja Peninsula
Gulf of California
Baja California Sur

Culiacán
MADRE
Torreón
Saltillo
SIERRA
Reynosa
Monterrey ● Matamoros
Brownsville

Durango
OCCIDENTAL
Mazatlán
MADRE

MEXICO

Aguascalientes
San Luis Potosi
Tepic
Tampico

Guadalajara ■
León
ORIENTAL

Morelia ● Mexico City
Toluca ▣
Popocatépetl ▲ Puebla
17,887'
(5452m)
Jalapa
Campeche Bay
Mérida

Veracruz
Yucatán
Peninsula

Acapulco
Oaxaca
Villahermosa
Belmopan
BEL

Tuxtla Gutiérrez
Sa
Pe
Su

GUATEMALA
Tapachula
Guatemala C
Quezaltenango ▣
Teguci

Santa Ana ▣
Sa
EL SALVADOR San
Salvador
M

PACIFIC OCEAN

miles
0   200   400   600
0   200   400   600   800
kilometers

30°
25°
20°
15°
10°
5°

115°
110°
105°
100°
95°
90°

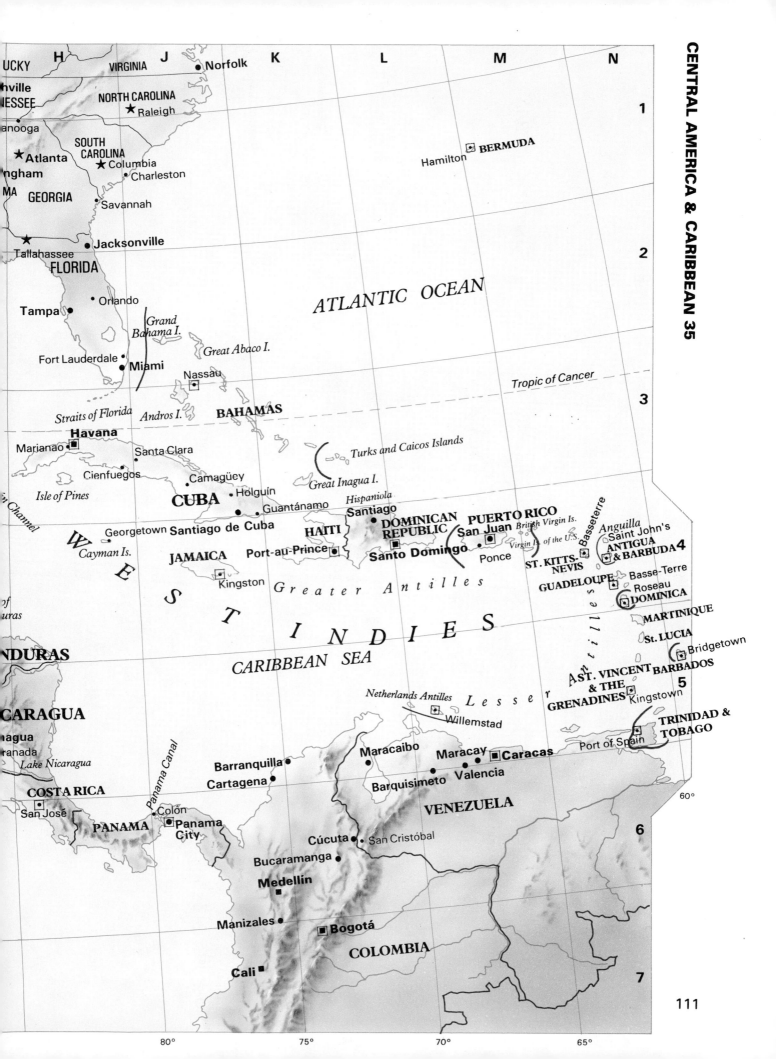

UCKY H   J   VIRGINIA   • Norfolk   K   L   M   N

hville

NESSEE

anooga

NORTH CAROLINA

★ Raleigh **1**

SOUTH
CAROLINA

★ Atlanta

ngham

★ Columbia

• Charleston

MA

GEORGIA

• Savannah

Hamilton ☐ **BERMUDA**

★ Tallahassee

• Jacksonville **2**

FLORIDA

ATLANTIC OCEAN

Tampa • Orlando

*Grand
Bahama I.*

Great Abaco I.

Fort Lauderdale • **Miami**

Nassau ☐

Tropic of Cancer **3**

Straits of Florida *Andros I.* **BAHAMAS**

Havana

Marianao ○ ☐

Turks and Caicos Islands

Santa Clara •

Great Inagua I.

• Cienfuegos • Camagüey

n Channel

Isle of Pines

CUBA • Holguín

Hispaniola

Santiago

**DOMINICAN
REPUBLIC**

PUERTO RICO

Basseterre

Anguilla

Guantánamo

HAITI

San Juan

British Virgin Is.

Saint John's

W

Georgetown **Santiago de Cuba**

Virgin Is. of the U.S.

**ANTIGUA
& BARBUDA 4**

Cayman Is.

E

JAMAICA

Port-au-Prince ☐

Santo Domingo

Ponce

**ST. KITTS-
NEVIS**

GUADELOUPE ☐ *Basse-Terre*

of

uras

S

T

Kingston ☐

G r e a t e r A n t i l l e s

• Roseau

☐ **DOMINICA**

I

MARTINIQUE

NDURAS

N

CARIBBEAN SEA

St. LUCIA

Bridgetown

D

L e s s e r

A **ST. VINCENT
& THE
GRENADINES**

BARBADOS **5**

CARAGUA

I

E

S

Netherlands Antilles

☐ Willemstad

A n t i l l e s

Kingstown

**TRINIDAD &
TOBAGO**

agua

Maracaibo

Maracay • ☐ **Caracas**

Port of Spain ☐

ranada

Lake Nicaragua

Barranquilla •

Barquisimeto • Valencia

COSTA RICA

Cartagena •

Panama Canal

VENEZUELA

60° *

San José ☐

Colón •

PANAMA ☐ Panama
City

Cúcuta • San Cristóbal **6**

Bucaramanga •

Medellín ■

Manizales •

☐ **Bogotá**

COLOMBIA

Cali ■ **7**

80°   75°   70°   65°

ATLANTIC OCEAN

CARIBBEAN SEA

Netherlands Antilles

PANAMA
Panamá Canal
Panamá City
Gulf of Panamá

Barranquilla
Cartagena
Ciénaga
Maracaibo
Cabimas
Maracay Caracas
Valencia
Barquisimeto
VENEZUELA
Cumaná
Port of Spain
TRINIDAD & TOBAGO

Valledupar
Montería
Cúcuta
Bucaramanga
San Cristóbal
San Fernando
Ciudad Guayana
Ciudad Bolivar
Orinoco
Caroni
Angel Falls

Georgetown
New Amsterdam
Paramaribo
Cayenne
FRENCH GUIANA
SURINAME
GUYANA
GUIANA HIGHLANDS

Medellín
Manizales
Pereira
Armenia
Ibagué
Cali
Palmira
Tunja
Bogotá
Neiva

COLOMBIA

Pasto
Quito
ECUADOR
Guayaquil
Cuenca
Chimborazo
20,577'(6272m)

Boa Vista

Negro

Macapá
Belém

Equator

São Luis
Teresina
Fortaleza

Natal
João Pessoa
Recife
Caruaru
Campina Grande
Maceió
Aracaju
Feira de Santana
Salvador
Itabuna
Governador Valad.

Amazon

Manaus

BRAZIL

Madeira
Tapajós
Xingu
Tocantins
Araguaia

Brasília
Goiânia
Uberlândia

BRAZILIAN HIGHLANDS

São Francisco

S e l v a s

Rio Branco

Iquitos
Marañón

Piura
Chiclayo
Trujillo
Chimbote
Huascaran
22,205'(6768m)
Callao
Lima
Cuzco
PERU

ANDES

Mato Grosso
Mato Grosso
Cuiabá
Paraguay

BOLIVIA
Santa Cruz
Cochabamba
Sucre
La Paz
Oruro
Lake Titicaca
Lake Poopó

Arequipa
Arica
Atacama

Rio de Janeiro
Niterói
Santo André
São
Paulo
Santos

SOUTH ATLANTIC
OCEAN

Florianópolis

Curitiba
Caxias do Sul
Pôrto Alegre

Londrina
Foz do Iguaçu
Rio Grande

Santa Mariá
Pelotas

Asunción
Uruguaiana
Salto
Paysandú
URUGUAY
Montevideo
Rio de la Plata

Corrientes
Concordia
La Plata
Mar del Plata

Resistencia

San Miguel de
Tucumán
Santa
Fé
Buenos Aires
Bahía Blanca

Salta
Córdoba
Rosario

Santiago
del Estero
P a m p a
ARGENTINA

San Juan
Mendoza
Comodoro
Rivadavia

ANDES
Aconcagua
(22,835'/6965m)
P a t a g o n i a

Desert
Valparaíso
Santiago
Rancagua

CHILE
Viña del Mar
Talca
Chillán

Antofagasta
Talcahuano
Concepción
Temuco
Valdivia
Puerto Montt

Stanley
Falkland Islands
(U.K.)

Strait of
Magellan
Tierra del
Fuego
Cape Horn

Punta Arenas

Tropic of Capricorn

San Ambrosio
(Chile)

PACIFIC

San Felix
OCEAN

Juan Fernández Is.
(Chile)

30°
40°
50°
60°
70°
80°
30°
40°
50°

5
6
7
8

miles
kilometers
0
200
400
600
200
400
600
800
1000

113

INDONESIA

Sumba

Timor

TIMOR SEA

Melville I.

• Darwin

ARNHEM LAND

Katherine

Groo Eyl

• Birdum

BARKLY TABLELA

Wyndham

KIMBERLEY PLATEAU

• Derby

Halls Creek

Broome

Tennant Creek

Great Sandy Desert

NORTHERN TERRITORY

AUSTRALIA

• Port Hedland

Dampier

HAMERSLEY RANGE

Newman • *Tropic of Capricorn*

MACDONNELL RANGE

• Alice Springs

Simpson Desert

BARLEE RANGE

Gibson Desert

▲ Ayers Rock 2844' (867m)

Carnarvon

MUSGRAVE RANGES

Lake

WESTERN AUSTRALIA

SOUTH AUSTRALIA

• Mount Magnet

Great Victoria Desert

Geraldton

• Woome

• Moora

• Kalgoorlie

Coolgardie

Nullarbor Plain

Eucla •

Ceduna

Port Augus

• Northam

Eyre Peninsula

Perth •

Fremantle

Mandurah

• Narrogin

Esperance

Great Australian Bight

Bunbury

Port Lincoln

Adel

• Augusta

Spencer Gulf

Albany

Kangaroo I.

INDIAN

OCEAN

miles
0   200   400

0   200   400   600
kilometers

115°   120°   125°   130°   135°

PAPUA NEW GUINEA

Port Moresby

G | H | J | K | L

1

Cape York

Solomon Islands

GREAT BARRIER REEF

GREAT DIVIDING RANGE

Cooktown

2

entaria

Normanton

Cairns

CORAL SEA

160° | 165°

Townsville • Bowen

3

unt Isa

Hughenden

Mackay

Winton

Great

Barcaldine

Rockhampton

4

QUEENSLAND

rtesian

Basin

Bundaberg

N | O

Maryborough

Charleville

35°

Kaitaia

Whangarei

5

Toowoomba • **Brisbane**

Goondiwindi

Gold Coast

Lismore

Auckland

North I.

Waihi

9

Bourke

Narrabri

Grafton

Hamilton

Tauranga

Rotorua

Opotiki

R. Darling

Nyngan

Tamworth

Port Macquarie

New Plymouth

Waitara

Taupo

Gisborne

Broken Hill

Dubbo

Taree

Lake Taupo

NEW SOUTH WALES

Orange

Newcastle

Mt Egmont
8620'(2518m)

Mt Ruapehu
9177'(2797m)

Napier

6

Katoomba

Sydney

Wanganui

Wagga Wagga

Wollongong

TASMAN SEA

Palmerston North

R. Murray

Canberra

155°

40°

Levin

Masterton

VICTORIA

Albury

GREAT

Mt Kosciusko
7305'
(2230m)

Nelson

Cook Strait

□ **Wellington**

Wangaratta

DIVIDING RANGE

Westport

Blenheim

Bendigo

Ballarat

NEW ZEALAND

unt ambier

■ **Melbourne**

Greymouth

South I.

10

arrnambool

Geelong • Morwell

7

SOUTHERN ALPS

SOUTH PACIFIC OCEAN

King I.

Bass Strait

Flinders I.

M

Mt Cook
12,349'
(3764m)

Christchurch

Timaru

Devonport

Launceston

Wanaka

Mt Ossa
5305
(1617m)

TASMANIA

Alexandra

Dunedin

8

Hobart

Gore

Balclutha

Invercargill

Stewart I.

miles
0 | 100 | 200 | 300

0 | 100 | 200 | 300 | 400
kilometers

11

145° | 150° | 170° | 175°

115

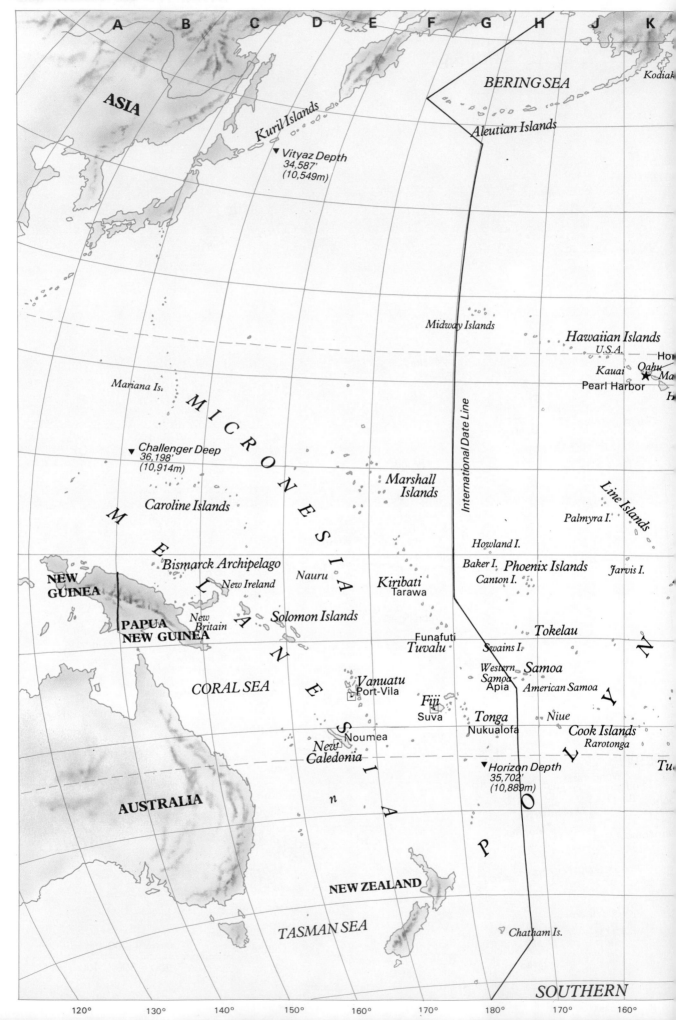

ASIA

A B C D E F G H J K

Kuril Islands

BERING SEA

Kodiak

Aleutian Islands

▼ *Vityaz Depth*
34,587'
(10,549m)

Midway Islands

Hawaiian Islands
U.S.A.

Ho
Kauai *Oahu* *Ma*
★
Pearl Harbor
H

Mariana Is.

M I C R O N E S I A

*Marshall
Islands*

Line Islands

▼ *Challenger Deep*
36,198'
(10,914m)

Caroline Islands

Palmyra I.

M
E
L
A
N
E
S
I
A

Howland I.

Bismarck Archipelago

Nauru

New Ireland

Kiribati
Tarawa

Baker I. **Phoenix Islands**
Canton I.

Jarvis I.

**NEW
GUINEA**

**PAPUA
NEW GUINEA**

*New
Britain*

Solomon Islands

Tokelau

Funafuti
Tuvalu

Swains I.

*Western
Samoa* **Samoa**
Apia *American Samoa*

CORAL SEA

Vanuatu
Port-Vila

Fiji
Suva

Tonga
Nukualofa

Niue

Cook Islands
Rarotonga

*New
Caledonia*
Noumea

▼ *Horizon Depth*
35,702'
(10,889m)

Tu

AUSTRALIA

n

P
O
L
Y
N

International Date Line

NEW ZEALAND

TASMAN SEA

Chatham Is.

SOUTHERN

120° 130° 140° 150° 160° 170° 180° 170° 160°

M N P Q R S ∧ T U 2

50° 40°

3

NORTH   AMERICA

30°

4

20°

Tropic of Cancer

5

A

Revilla Gigedo Is.   CENTRAL
AMERICA

10°

Clipperton I.

6

Equator

Galápagos Islands

0°

SOUTH
AMERICA

7

Marquesas Is

10°

Tuamotu Archipelago

ea
hiti
iety   FRENCH
nds   POLYNESIA

8

Gambier Is.   Tropic of Capricorn

nds   *Pitcairn I.*

20°

Easter I.

9

Juan Fernández

miles
0   500   1000   1500

30°

0   500 1000 1500 2000
kilometers

10

AN

140°   130°   120°   110°   100°   90°   80°   70°

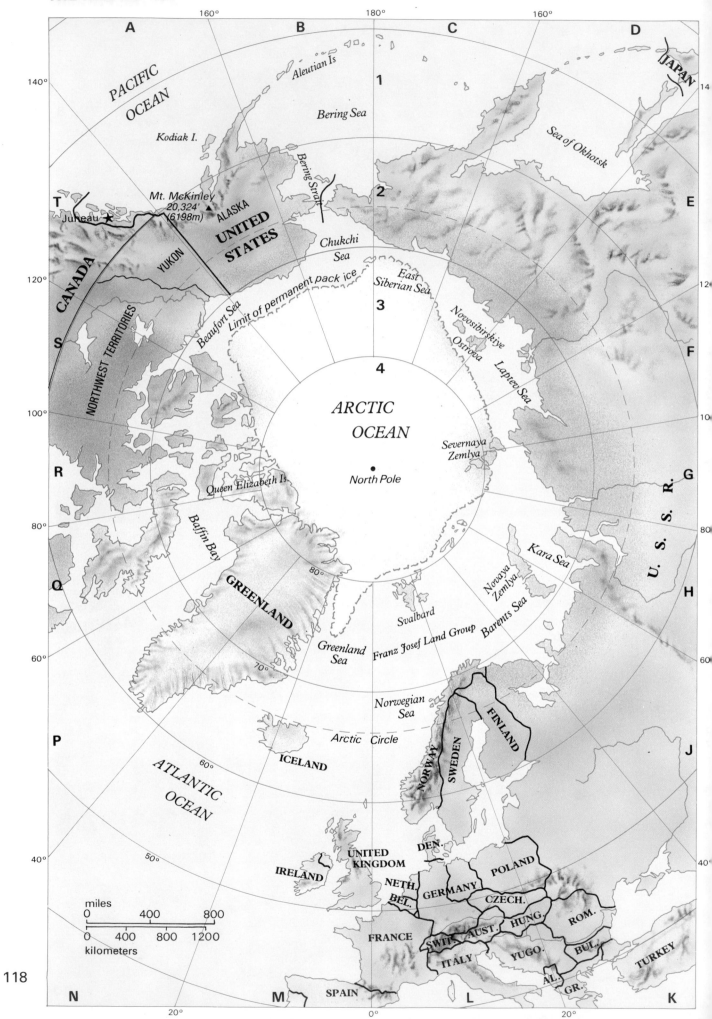

THE ARCTIC 42

A
140°
160°
B
180°
C
160°
D
14

1
2
3
4

PACIFIC OCEAN

Aleutian Is.

Bering Sea

Kodiak I.

Bering Strait

Sea of Okhotsk

JAPAN

T
Mt. McKinley
20,324'
(6198m)
ALASKA
UNITED STATES

Juneau

CANADA

YUKON

120°

S

NORTHWEST TERRITORIES

Beaufort Sea

Limit of permanent pack ice

Chukchi Sea

East Siberian Sea

Novosibirskiye Ostrova

Laptev Sea

E
12

F
10

ARCTIC OCEAN

North Pole

Severnaya Zemlya

R
100°

Queen Elizabeth Is.

G

Q
80°

Baffin Bay

GREENLAND

80°

Kara Sea

Novaya Zemlya

Barents Sea

U. S. S. R.

80°

H

Svalbard

Franz Josef Land Group

Greenland Sea

60°

70°

Norwegian Sea

P

ATLANTIC OCEAN

60°

Arctic Circle

ICELAND

NORWAY

SWEDEN

FINLAND

J

IRELAND

UNITED KINGDOM

DEN.

POLAND

40°

40°

NETH.
BEL.

GERMANY

CZECH.

FRANCE

SWIT. AUST. HUNG.

ROM.

ITALY

YUGO.

BUL.

TURKEY

K

AL.

GR.

SPAIN

miles
0   400   800
0 400 800 1200
kilometers

118

N
20°
M
0°
L
20°
K

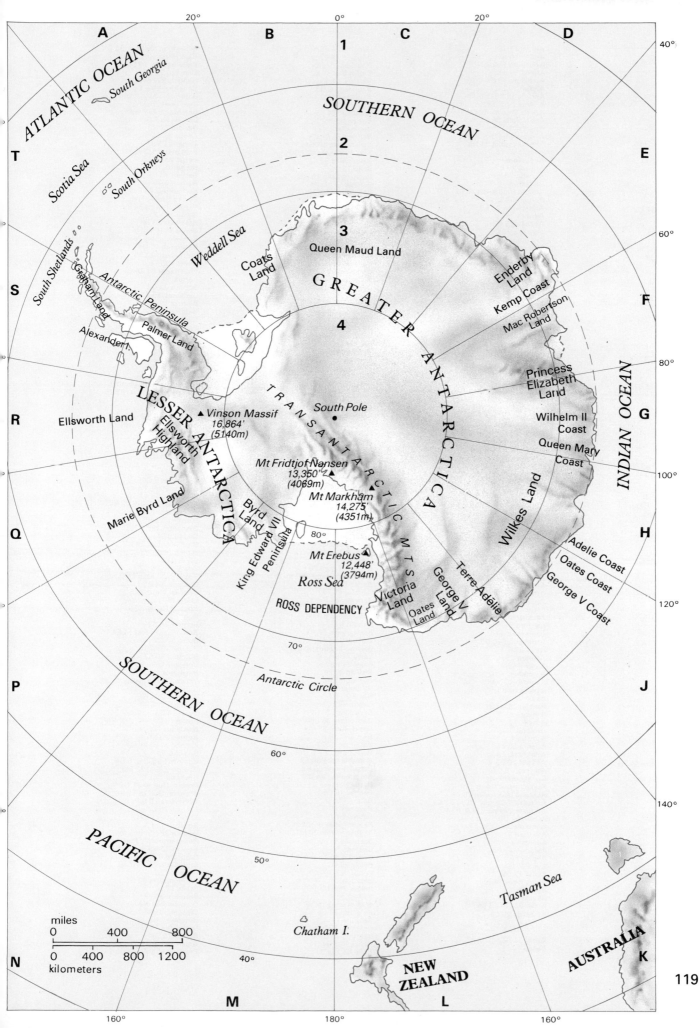

ATLANTIC OCEAN

SOUTHERN OCEAN

South Georgia

Scotia Sea

South Orkneys

Weddell Sea

Queen Maud Land

Coats Land

GREATER ANTARCTICA

Enderby Land

Kemp Coast

Mac Robertson Land

South Shetlands

Graham Land

Antarctic Peninsula

Palmer Land

Alexander I.

Princess Elizabeth Land

Wilhelm II Coast

Queen Mary Coast

LESSER ANTARCTICA

Ellsworth Land

▲ Vinson Massif
16,864'
(5140m)

South Pole

Ellsworth Highland

Mt Fridtjof Nansen
13,350' ▲
(4069m)

Mt Markham
14,275'
(4351m)

Marie Byrd Land

Byrd Land

King Edward VII Peninsula

Mt Erebus ▲
12,448'
(3794m)

Ross Sea

ROSS DEPENDENCY

Victoria Land

T R A N S A N T A R C T I C   M T S

George V Land

Oates Land

Terre Adélie

Adélie Coast

Oates Coast

George V Coast

Wilkes Land

INDIAN OCEAN

SOUTHERN OCEAN

Antarctic Circle

PACIFIC OCEAN

Chatham I.

Tasman Sea

NEW ZEALAND

AUSTRALIA

miles
0   400   800

0   400   800   1200
kilometers

40° 20° 0° 20° 40° 60° 80° 100° 120° 140° 160° 180° 160°

A B 1 C D E F G H J K L M N P Q R S T

20° 30° 40° 50° 60° 70° 80°

MAP INDEX

Lourdes 10 D5
Lower Lough Erne 9 D2
Lowestoft 6 J4
Loyang 25 H4
Luanda 29 F5
Luang Prabang 26 B2
Luanshya 29 G6
Lubango 29 F6
Lübeck 14 D2
Lublin 15 K3
Lubumbashi 29 G6
Lucknow 22 E3
Ludhiana 22 D2
Lugo 12 C1
Lugoj 17 H2
Lule 13 H5
Luleå 13 H5
Luleburgaz 17 L4
Lurgan 9 E2
Lusaka 29 G6
Lü-ta 25 K3
Luton 7 G5
Luxembourg 14 B4
Luxor 20 B4
Luzern 11 J3
Luzon 27 F2
Luzon Strait 27 F2
Lvov 18 C5
Lyon 11 G4

M
Maas 14 A3
Maastricht 14 A3
Macao 25 H6
Macapá 36 D2
M'Clintock Channel 30 F2
McClure Strait 30 E2
Macdonnell Range 38 E4
Maceió 36 F3
Machilipatnam 22 E5
Mackay 39 H4
Mackenzie 30 D4
Mackenzie Mts. 30 C4
McKinley, Mt. 30 A4
Macomer 16 B4
Mâcon 11 G3
Mac Robertson Land 43 F2
Madagascar 29 J7
Madeira 28 C1
Madeira R. 36 C3
Madison 33 J3
Madras 22 E6
Madrid 12 E2
Madurai 22 D7
Mafikeng 28 N9
Magadan 19 J4
Magdeburg 14 D2
Magellan, Strait of 37 C8
Maggiore, Lake 16 B2
Magnitogorsk 18 D4
Mahajanga 29 J6
Maidstone 7 H5
Maiduguri 29 F3
Main 14 D3
Maine 33 N2
Mainz 14 C4
Majene 26 E6
Majorca 12 H3
Makassar Strait 26 E6
Makhachkala 18 D5
Malabo 29 E4
Malacca, Strait of 26 B5
Málaga 12 D4
Malang 26 D7
Malange 29 F5
Mälaren, Lake 13 G7
Malatya 20 C2
Malawi 29 H6
Malawi, Lake 29 H6
Malaysia 26
Malbork 15 H1
Malegaon 22 C4
Mali 28 D3
Mallow 9 C4
Malmö 13 F7
Malta 16 E7
Manado 27 F5
Managua 35 G5
Manama 21 F4
Manaus 36 D3
Manchester 6 E3
Mandala Peak 27 K6
Mandalay 23 H4
Mandurah 38 B6
Mangalia 17 M3
Mangalore 22 C6
Manila 26 F3
Manisa 17 L5
Manitoba 30 G5
Manizales 36 B2
Mansfield 6 F3
Maoke Range 27 J6
Maputo 28 P9
Maracaibo 36 B1
Maracay 36 C1
Maragheh 20 E2
Marañón 36 B3
Maras 20 C2
Marathon 17 J5
Marbella 12 D4
Mar del Plata 37 D6
Mardin 20 D2
Margate 7 J5
Marianao 35 H3

Mariana Is. 40 D5
Maribor 16 E1
Maritsa 17 K3
Marmara, Sea of 17 M4
Marmaris 17 M6
Marne 11 F2
Marquesas Is. 41 M7
Marrakech 28 D1
Marseille 11 G5
Marshall Is. 40 G6
Martaban, Gulf of 23 H5
Martinique 35 M5
Maryborough 39 J5
Maryland 33 L4
Masan 25 L3
Maseru 28 N9
Mashhad 21 G2
Mask, Lough 9 B3
Massachusetts 33 M3
Massawa 29 H3
Massif Central 11 F4
Masterton 39 O10
Masvingo 29 H7
Matadi 29 F5
Matamoros 34 E2
Mathura 22 D3
Mato Grosso 36 D4
Matruh 20 A3
Matsuyama 25 M4
Matterhorn 16 A2
Maui 40 K4
Mauritania 28 C3
Mazar-i-Sharif 21 J2
Mazatlán 34 C3
Mbabane 28 P9
Mbandaka 29 F4
Mbuju Mayi 29 G5
Mecca 20 C5
Medan 26 A5
Medellín 36 B2
Medina 20 C5
Meerut 22 D3
Meissen 14 E3
Meknès 28 D1
Mekong 26 B2
Melbourne 39 G7
Melville I. (Australia) 38 E2
Melville I. (Canada) 30 E1
Memmingen 14 D5
Memphis 33 J4
Mendi 27 K7
Mendoza 37 C6
Merauke 27 K7
Mergui Archipelago 23 H6
Mérida (Mexico) 34 G3
Mérida (Spain) 12 C3
Mersin 20 B2
Merthyr Tydfil 7 D5
Meseta 4 C4
Mesolóngion 17 H5
Messina 16 E5
Metković 16 F3
Metz 11 H2
Meuse 11 G1
Mexicali 34 A1
Mexico 34
Mexico, Gulf of 34 F2
Mexico City 34 E4
Mezenc, Mt. 11 G4
Miami 35 H2
Michigan 33 J2
Michigan, Lake 33 J3
Micronesia 40
Middlesbrough and Teeside 6 F2
Midway Is. 40 H4
Midye 17 M4
Milan 16 B2
Milâs 17 L6
Milford Haven 7 B5
Milos 17 K6
Milton Keynes 7 G5
Milwaukee 33 J3
Mindanao 27 G4
Mindoro 26 F3
Minna 29 E4
Minneapolis 33 H2
Minnesota 33 H2
Minorca 12 J3
Minsk 18 C4
Miquelon 31 L7
Mirzapur 23 E3
Miskolc 15 J4
Misool 27 H6
Mississippi 33 J5
Mississippi R. 33 H3
Missouri 33 H4
Missouri R. 32 E2
Misurata 29 F1
Mitchell, Mt. 33 K4
Mitilini 17 L5
Miyazaki 25 M4
Mobile 33 J5
Moçambique 29 J6
Modena 16 C2
Moffat 8 E5
Mogadishu 29 J4
Moluccas 27 G6
Mombasa 29 H5
Monaco 16 A3
Monaghan 9 E2
Mönchen-Gladbach 14 B3
Moncton 31 K7
Monghyr 23 F3
Mongolia 19 G5
Mongu 29 G6

Monroe 33 H5
Monrovia 28 C4
Mons 11 F1
Montana 32 E2
Montargis 11 F3
Montauban 10 E5
Montélimar 11 G4
Monteria 36 B2
Monterrey 34 D2
Montevideo 37 D6
Montgomery 33 J5
Montluçon 11 F3
Montpellier 11 F5
Montreal 31 J7
Montreux 11 H3
Montrose 8 F4
Monza 16 B2
Moora 38 B6
Moorea 41 L8
Moose Jaw 30 F6
Mora 13 F6
Moradabad 22 D3
Morant 38 B5
Morecambe 6 E2
Morelia 34 D4
Morlaix 10 C2
Morocco 28 D1
Morwell 39 H7
Moscow 18 C4
Mosel 14 B4
Mossel Bay 28 M10
Mostar 16 F3
Mosul 20 D2
Motala 13 F7
Motherwell 8 E5
Moulmein 23 H5
Mount Gambier 39 G7
Mount Isa 39 F4
Mount Magnet 38 B5
Mount Newman 38 B4
Mozambique 29 H6
Mozambique Channel 29 J6
Mudanjiang 25 L2
Mukachevo 15 K4
Mulhacén 12 E4
Mulhouse 11 H3
Mull 8 C4
Multan 22 C2
Munich 14 D4
Münster 14 B3
Murcia 12 F4
Mures 17 J1
Murmansk 18 C3
Murray 39 G7
Murud 26 E5
Muscat 21 G5
Musgrave Ranges 38 E5
Mutare 29 H6
Muzaffarpur 23 F3
Mwanza 29 H5
Myingyan 23 H4
Myitkyina 23 H3
Mysore 22 D6
My Tho 26 C3

N
Naas 9 E3
Nagasaki 25 L4
Nagercoil 22 D7
Nagoya 25 N3
Nagpur 22 D4
Nagykanizsa 15 G5
Naha 25 L5
Nain 31 K5
Nairn 8 E3
Nairobi 29 H5
Nakhodka 19 H5
Nakhon Ratchasima 26 B2
Nakhon Sawan 26 B2
Nakuru 29 H5
Namibia 28 L9
Namib Desert 28 L8
Nampula 29 H6
Namur 11 G1
Nanchang 25 J5
Nancy 11 H2
Nanda Devi 22 E2
Nander 22 D5
Nanga Parbat 22 C1
Nanking 25 J4
Nanning 24 G6
Nantes 10 D3
Napier 39 O9
Naples 16 E4
Narayanganj 23 G4
Narbonne 11 F5
Narodnaya 18 E3
Narrabri 39 H6
Narrogin 38 B6
Narva 13 J7
Narvik 13 G5
Nashville 33 J4
Nasik 22 C5
Nassau 35 J2
Nasser, Lake 20 B5
Natal 36 F3
Návpaktos 17 H5
Návplion 17 H6
Náxos 17 K6
N'Djamena 29 F3
Ndola 29 G6
Neagh, Lough 9 E2
Nebraska 32 G3
Negoiu 17 K2

Negro 36 C3
Negros 27 F4
Neisse 15 F3
Neiva 36 B2
Nellore 22 E6
Nenagh 9 C4
Nene 6 G4
Nepal 23 E3
Ness, Loch 8 D3
Netherlands 14
Neubrandenburg 14 E2
Neuchâtel 11 H3
Neuchâtel, Lac de 11 H3
Neumünster 14 C1
Neusiedler, Lake 15 G5
Nevada 32 C3
Nevis 35 M4
New Amsterdam 36 D2
Newark 33 M3
Newark-on-Trent 6 G3
New Britain 40 E7
New Brunswick 31 K7
New Caledonia 40 F9
Newcastle 39 J6
Newcastle-under-Lyme 6 E3
Newcastle-upon-Tyne 6 F1
New Delhi 22 D3
Newfoundland 31 L7
New Guinea 40 D7
New Hampshire 33 M3
New Ireland 40 E7
New Jersey 33 M3
New Mexico 32 E5
New Orleans 33 J6
New Plymouth 39 N9
Newport (England) 7 F6
Newport (Wales) 7 E5
Newquay 7 B6
New Ross 9 E4
Newry 9 E2
New Siberian Is. 19 J2
New South Wales 39 H6
Newton 6 D4
Newton Stewart 8 D6
Newtonabbey 9 F2
New York 33 M3
New Zealand 39 N10
Nha Trang 26 C3
Niagara Falls 31 J8
Niamey 28 E3
Nias 26 A5
Nicaragua 35 H5
Nicaragua, Lake 35 G5
Nice 11 H5
Nicobar Is. 23 G7
Nicosia 20 B2
Niger 29 F3
Niger, R. 28 D3
Nigeria 29 E4
Niigata 25 N3
Nikšić 17 G3
Nile 20 B4
Nîmes 11 G5
Ningpo 25 K5
Nis 17 H3
Niterói 37 E5
Nizhniy Tagil 18 D4
Noirmoutier, Île de 10 C3
Nordvik 19 G2
Norfolk 33 L4
Norilsk 18 F3
Normanton 39 G3
Norrköping 13 G7
Northam 38 B6
Northampton 7 G4
North Bay 31 J7
North Cape 13 J4
North Carolina 33 L4
North Channel 6 B2
North Dakota 32 F2
North Downs 7 H5
Northern Ireland 9 E2
Northern Territory 38 E4
North I. 39 O9
North Pole 42
North Sea 4 G2
North Uist 8 A3
North West Highlands 8 C3
Northwest Territories 30 E4
North York Moors 6 F2
Norway 13
Norwegian Sea 4 C2
Norwich 6 J4
Nottingham 6 F4
Nouadhibou 28 C2
Nouakchott 28 C3
Novara 16 B2
Nova Scotia 31 K8
Nova Siberia 19 J2
Novaya Zemlya 18 D2
Novgorod 18 C4
Novi Sad 17 G2
Novokuznetsk 18 F4
Novosibirsk 18 F4
Novosibirskiye 42 D3
Nubian Desert 20 B5
Nuevo Laredo 34 E2
Nullarbor Plain 38 D6
Nuremberg 14 D4
Nyngan 39 H6

O
Oahu 40 K4

Oakland 32 B4
Oates Land 43 K3
Oaxaca 34 E4
Ob 18 F4
Oban 8 C4
Obi 27 G6
October Revolution I. 19 F2
Odda 13 E6
Odense 13 F7
Oder 15 F2
Odessa 18 C5
Offenbach 14 C3
Offenburg 14 B4
Ogbomosho 28 jE4
Ogden 32 D3
Ogulin 16 E2
Ohio 33 K3
Ohio, R 33 J4
Ohrid 17 H4
Ohridsko, Lake 17 H4
Okayama 25 M4
Okehampton 7 D6
Okha 19 J4
Okhotsk, Sea of 19 J4
Oklahoma 32 G4
Oklahoma City 32 G4
Öland 13 G7
Olbia 16 B4
Oldenburg 14 C2
Oldham 6 E3
Oléron, Ile d' 10 D4
Olomouc 15 G4
Olsztyn 15 J2
Olympia 32 B2
Olympus, Mt. 17 J4
Omagh 9 D2
Omaha 33 G3
Oman 21 G5
Oman, Gulf of 21 G5
Omdurman 20 B6
Omsk 18 E4
Onega, Lake 18 C3
Onitsha 28 E4
Ontario 31 H6
Ontario, Lake 33 L3
Oporto 12 B2
Opotiki 39 O9
Oradea 17 H1
Oran 28 D1
Orange 39 H6
Orange R. 28 L9
Ordzhonikidze 18 D5
Oregon 32 B3
Orel 18 C4
Ore Mts. 14 E3
Orenburg 18 D4
Orense 12 C1
Orinoco 36 C2
Oristano 16 B5
Orkney Is. 8 F1
Orlando 35 H2
Orléans 11 E3
Orsk 18 D4
Oruro 36 C4
Osaka 25 N4
Osh 18 E5
Oshogbo 28 F4
Osijek 17 G2
Oslo 13 F7
Osnabrück 14 C2
Osorno 12 D1
Ossa, Mt. 39 H8
Ostend 11 F1
Östersund 13 F6
Ostrava 15 H4
Otranto 17 G4
Otranto, Strait of 17 G4
Ottawa 31 J7
Ouagadougou 28 D3
Oudtshoorn 28 M10
Ouessant, Ile d' 10 B2
Oujda 28 D1
Oulu 13 J5
Ouse 6 F2
Outer Hebrides 8 A3
Oviedo 12 D1
Oxford 7 F5

P
Paarl 28 L10
Padang 26 B6
Padua 16 C2
Paisley 8 D5
Pakanbaru 26 B5
Pakistan 22 B3
Pakse 26 C2
Palawan 26 E4
Palembang 26 B6
Palencia 12 D1
Palermo 16 D5
Palma 12 H3
Palmer Land 43 S3
Palmerston North 39 O10
Palmira 36 B2
Pampas 37 C6
Pamplona 12 F1
Panama 35 H6
Panamá, Gulf of 36 B2
Panama Canal 35 J6
Panama City 35 J6
Panay 27 F3
Pantelleria 16 C6
Paoki 24 G4

Paoting 25 J3
Paotow 25 G2
Papua, Gulf of 27 K7
Papua New Guinea 27 K7
Paraguay 37 D5
Paraguay R. 36 D4
Paramaribo 36 D2
Paraná 37 D5
Paris 11 F2
Parkano 13 H6
Parma 16 C2
Pasto 36 B2
Patagonia 37 C7
Patiala 22 D2
Patna 23 F3
Pátras 17 H5
Pau 10 D5
Pavlodar 18 E4
Paysandú 37 D6
Pearl Harbor 40 K5
Pec 17 H3
Pechenga 13 K5
Pechora 5 J1
Pécs 15 H5
Peebles 8 E5
Pegu 23 H5
Peking 25 J3
Pelotas 37 D6
Pematangsiantar 26 A5
Pemba 29 J6
Pemba I. 29 H5
Pembroke 7 C5
Pengpu 25 J4
Penki 25 K2
Pennines 6 E2
Pennsylvania 33 L3
Penrith 6 E2
Penzance 7 B6
Penza 18 D4
Peoria 33 J3
Pereira 36 B2
Périgueux 10 E4
Perm 18 D4
Perpignan 11 F5
Persian Gulf 20 E4
Perth (Australia) 38 B6
Perth (Scotland) 8 E4
Peru 36 B4
Pescara 16 E3
Peshawar 22 C2
Peterborough (Canada) 31 J8
Peterborough (England) 6 G4
Peterhead 8 G3
Petrich 17 J4
Petropavlovsk 18 E4
Petropavlovsk Kamchatskiy 19 J4
Patrópolis 37 E5
Petrozavodsk 18 C3
Philadelphia 33 L3
Philippines 27
Phnom Penh 26 B3
Phoenix 32 D5
Phoenix Is. 40 H7
Phuket 26 A4
Pierre 32 F3
Pietermaritzburg 28 P9
Pietersburg 28 N8
Pila 15 G2
Pilos 17 H6
Pindus Mts. 17 H5
Pines, I. of 35 H3
Piraeus 17 J6
Pírgos 17 H6
Pisa 16 C3
Pitcairn I. 41 M9
Pitesti 17 K2
Pitlochry 8 E4
Pittsburgh 33 L3
Piura 36 A3
Plateau of Tibet 23 E2
Pleven 17 K3
Ploesti 17 L2
Plovdiv 17 K3
Plymouth 7 C6
Plzen 14 E4
Po 16 C2
Pointe Noire 29 F5
Poitiers 10 E3
Poland 15
Polynesia 40
Ponce 35 L4
Pontianak 26 C6
Pontine Mts. 20 C1
Pontypool 7 D5
Pontypridd 7 D5
Poole 7 F6
Poopó, Lak 36 C4
Popocatépetl 34 E4
Portadown 9 E2
Port Arthur 33 H5
Port Augusta 38 F6
Port-au-Prince 35 K4
Port Bou 12 H1
Port Elizabeth 28 N10
Port-Gentil 29 E5
Port Harcourt 28 E4
Port Hedland 38 B4
Portland 32 B2
Portlaoighise 9 D3
Port Lincoln 38 F6
Port Macquarie 39 J6
Port Moresby (New Guinea) 40 A7
Pórto Alegre 37 D5

Port of Spain 36 C1
Porto-Novo 28 E4
Port Pirie 38 F6
Portree 8 B3
Portrush 9 E1
Port Said 20 B3
Portsmouth 7 F6
Port Sudan 20 C6
Port Talbot 7 D5
Portugal 12
Po-Shan 25 J3
Potchefstroom 28 N9
Potosí 36 C4
Potsdam 14 E2
Poznań 15 G2
Prague 15 F3
Prespa, Lake 17 H4
Preston 6 E3
Prestwick 8 D5
Pretoria 28 N9
Préveza 17 H5
Prince Charles I. 31 J3
Prince Edward I. 31 K7
Prince George 30 D6
Prince of Wales I. 30 G2
Princess Elizabeth Land 43 G3
Principe 29 E4
Pristina 17 H3
Prokopyevsk 18 F4
Providence 33 M3
Provo 32 D3
Przemyśl 15 K4
Pskov 18 C4
Puebla 34 E4
Pueblo 32 F4
Puerto Montt 37 B7
Puerto Rico 35 L4
Pultusk 15 J2
Puncak Jaya 27 J6
Pune 22 C5
Punta Arenas 37 B8
Pusan 25 L3
Pwllheli 6 C4
Pyongyang 25 L3
Pyrénées 12 G1

Q
Qahremanshahr 20 E3
Qatar 21 F4
Qattara Depression 29 G2
Qazvin 20 E2
Qishn 21 F6
Qom 21 F3
Quebec 31 J7
Queen Charlotte Is. 30 C6
Queen Mary Coast 43 G2
Queen Maud Land 43 C3
Queensland 39 G4
Queenstown 28 N10
Quetta 22 B2
Quezaltenango 34 F5
Quezon City 27 F3
Quimper 10 B3
Qui Nhon 26 C3
Quito 36 B3

R
Raba 26 E7
Rabat 28 D1
Rach Gia 26 C3
Radom 15 J3
Raipur 22 E4
Rajkot 22 C4
Raleigh 33 L4
Ramah 20 E4
Rampur 22 D3
Ramsgate 7 J5
Rancagua 37 B6
Ranchi 23 F4
Randers 13 F7
Rangoon 23 H5
Rantekombola 26 F6
Rarotonga 40 J9
Rasht 20 E2
Ratlam 22 D4
Rauma 13 H6
Ravenna 16 D2
Rawalpindi 22 C2
Razgrad 17 L3
Ré, Ile de 10 D3
Reading 7 G5
Recife 36 F3
Red R. (USA) 33 G5
Red R. (Vietnam) 26 B1
Red Sea 20
Ree, Lough 9 C3
Regensburg 14 E4
Reggio di Calabria 16 E5
Regina 30 F6
Reims 11 F2
Rennes 10 D2
Reno 32 C4
Resistencia 37 D5
Réthimnon 17 K7
Revilla Gigedo Is. 41 P5
Rey 21 F2
Reykjavik 13 A2
Reynosa 34 E2
Rezaiyeh 20 E2
Rhine 14 B3
Rhode Island 33 M3

Rhodes 17 M6
Rhodes (I.) 17 L6
Rhodope Mts. 17 J4
Rhondda 7 D5
Rhum 8 B4
Ribeirão Prêto 37 E5
Richmond 33 L4
Riga 18 C4
Rijeka 16 E2
Rimini 16 D2
Rio Branco 36 C3
Rio de Janeiro 37 E5
Rio Grande 34 E2
Ripon 6 F2
Riyadh 20 E5
Roccella 16 F5
Rochdale 6 E3
Rochester 33 L3
Rockhampton 39 J4
Rocky Mts. 30
Rohtak 22 D3
Romania 17
Rome 16 D4
Rosa, Monte 16 A2
Rosario 37 C6
Roscommon 9 C3
Roscrea 9 D4
Roskilde 13 F7
Ross Dependency 43 M3
Ross Sea 43 M3
Rostock 14 E1
Rostov 18 C5
Rotherham 6 F3
Rotorua 39 O9
Rotterdam 14 A3
Roubaix 11 F1
Rouen 10 E2
Rovno 18 C4
Rub al Khali 20 E6
Rugby 7 F4
Runcorn 6 E3
Ruse 17 K3
Rwanda 29 G5
Ryazan 18 C4
Ryde 7 F6
Rysy 15 J4
Ryukyu Is. 25 L5
Rzeszów 15 K3

S
Saarbrücken 14 B4
Saaremaa 13 H7
Sabadell 12 H2
Sabah 26 E4
Sacramento 32 B4
Safi 28 D1
Sahara 28 E2
Saharan Atlas 28 E1
Saharanpur 22 D3
Sahiwal 22 C2
St. Albans 7 G5
St. Andrews 8 F4
St. Austell 7 C6
St. Brieuc 10 C2
St. Elias Mtn. 30 A5
St. Etienne 11 G4
St. George's Channel 7 A5
St. Helens 6 E3
St. Helens, Mt. 32 B2
St. Helier 10 C2
St. John 31 K7
St. Johns 31 L7
St. Kitts 35 M4
St. Lawrence 31 K7
St. Lawrence, Gulf of 31 K7
St. Louis 33 H4
St. Lucia 35 M5
St. Malo 10 C2
St. Moritz 16 B1
St. Nazaire 10 C3
St. Paul 33 H3
St. Peter Port 7 E7
St. Pierre 31 L7
St. Polten 15 F4
St. Quentin 11 F2
St. Vincent and the
  Grenadines 35 M5
Sakhalin 19 J4
Salala 21 F6
Salamanca 12 D2
Salekhard 18 E3
Salem (India) 22 D6
Salem (USA) 32 B3
Salerno 16 E4
Salisbury 7 F5
Salmon River Mts. 32 C3
Salta 37 C5
Saltillo 34 D2
Salt Lake City 32 D3
Salto 37 D6
Salvador 36 F4
Salzburg 14 E5
Salzgitter 14 D2
Samar 27 G3
Samarinda 26 E6
Samarkand 18 E6
Samoa 40 H8
Sámos 17 L6
Samothráki 17 K4
Samsun 20 C1
Sana 20 D6
San Ambrosio 37 B5
San Antonio 32 G6
San Bernardino 32 C5

San Cristóbal 36 B2
San Diego 32 C5
Sandringham 6 H4
San Felix 37 A5
San Fernando 36 C2
San Francisco 32 B4
San Jose (Costa Rica) 35 H6
San Jose (USA) 32 B4
San Juan (Argentina) 37 C6
San Juan (Puerto Rico) 35 L4
San Luis Potosi 34 D3
San Marino 16 D3
San Miguel 34 G5
San Miguel de Tucumán 37 C5
San Pablo 27 F3
San Pedro Sula 34 G4
San Salvador 34 G5
San Sebastián 12 F1
Santa Ana 34 G5
Santa Barbara 32 C5
Santa Clara 35 J3
Santa Cruz 36 C4
Santa Fe 32 E4
Santa Fé 37 C6
Santa María 37 D5
Santander 12 E1
Santarém 12 B3
Santiago (Chile) 37 B6
Santiago (Dom. Rep.) 35 K4
Santiago 12 B1
Santiago de Cuba 35 J3
Santiago del Estero 37 C5
Santo André 37 E5
Santo Domingo 35 L4
Santos 37 E5
São Francisco 36 E4
São José do Rio Prêto 36 E5
São Luís 36 E3
Saône 11 G3
São Paulo 37 E5
São Tomé 28 E4
Sapporo 25 O2
Sarajevo 17 G3
Saratov 18 D4
Sarawak 26 D5
Sardinia 16 B4
Sargodha 22 C2
Sark 10 C2
Saskatchewan 30 F6
Saskatchewan R. 30 F6
Saskatoon 30 F6
Sássari 16 B4
Satu Mare 17 J1
Saudi Arabia 20
Sault Sainte Marie 31 H7
Sava 16 F2
Savannah 33 K5
Scafell Pike 6 D2
Scarborough 6 G2
Schwerin 14 D2
Scilly Is. 7 A7
Scotia Sea 43 T1
Scotland 8
Scunthorpe 6 G3
Seattle 32 B2
Segovia 12 D2
Seine 11 F2
Sekondi-Takoradi 28 D4
Selkirk Mts. 30 E6
Selvas 36 C3
Semarang 26 D7
Semipalatinsk 18 F4
Sendai 25 O3
Sénégal 28 C3
Senegal 28 C3
Senja 13 G5
Sennar 20 B7
Seoul 25 L3
Serov 18 E4
Sérrai 17 J4
Setúbal 12 B3
Severn 6 D4
Severnaya Zemlya 19 F2
Seville 12 D4
Seward 30 B4
Seydhisfjördhur 13 C2
Sfax 29 F1
Shah Fuladi 21 J3
Shahjahanpur 22 D3
Shanghai 25 K4
Shannon 9 D3
Shantar Is. 19 H4
Shaoyang 25 H5
Sharjah 21 G4
Sheffield 6 F3
Shëngjin 17 G4
Shenyang 25 K2
Shetland Is. 8 A1
Shihkiachwang 25 H3
Shikoku 25 M4
Shilka 19 G4
Shin, Loch 8 D2
Shiraz 21 F4
Shizuoka 25 N4
Shkodër 17 G3
Shkodër, Lake 17 G3
Sholapur 22 D5
Shreveport 33 H5
Shrewsbury 6 E4
Shwebo 23 H4
Sialkot 22 C2
Sian 25 G4
Siangtan 25 H5
Siauliai 13 H7

Siberut 26 A6
Sibu 26 D5
Sicily 16 D6
Sidi-bel-Abbès 28 D1
Siedlce 15 K2
Siegen 14 C3
Sierra Leone 28 C4
Sierra Madre Occidental 34 C2
Sierra Madre Oriental 34 E3
Sierra Morena 12 D3
Sierra Nevada (Spain) 12 E4
Sierra Nevada (USA) 32 C4
Siglufjördhur 13 B1
Siirt 20 D2
Si Kiang 25 H6
Silgarhi 22 E3
Silistra 17 L2
Simeulue 26 A5
Simferopol' 18 C5
Simpson Desert 38 F4
Sines 12 B4
Singapore 26 B5
Sining 24 F3
Sinop 20 C1
Sintang 26 D5
Sioux City 33 G3
Sioux Falls 33 G3
Siracusa 16 E6
Sisophon 26 B3
Sittwe 23 G4
Sivas 20 C2
Skagerrak 13 E7
Skagway 30 C5
Skegness 6 H3
Skellefteå 13 H6
Skíros 17 K5
Skopje 17 H3
Skye 8 B3
Slagelse 13 F7
Sligo 9 C2
Slough 7 G5
Smöla 13 E6
Smolyan 17 K4
Snaefell 6 C2
Snake 32 D3
Snåsa 13 F6
Snowdon 6 C3
Society Is. 41 L8
Sofia 17 J3
Sogne Fjord 13 E6
Söke 17 L6
Sokoto 28 E3
Solomon Is. 40 E7
Solway Firth 6 D2
Somalia 29 J4
Sombor 17 G2
Somerset I. 30 G2
Somme 11 F1
Songkhla 26 B4
Soochow 25 K4
Söröya 13 H4
Sortavala 13 K6
South Africa 28 M10
South America 36
Southampton 7 F6
Southampton I. 31 H4
South Atlantic Ocean 37 F6
South Australia 38 E5
South Carolina 33 K5
South China Sea 26 D3
South Dakota 32 F3
South Downs 7 G6
Southend 7 H5
Southern Alps 39 N10
Southern Ocean 43
Southern Uplands 8 D5
South Georgia 43 A1
South I. 39 N10
South Orkneys 43 T2
South Pacific Ocean 39 O10
South Pole 43
Southport 6 D3
South Shetlands 43 T2
South Shields 6 F2
South Uist 8 A3
Soweto 28 N9
Spain 12
Spalding 6 G4
Spencer Gulf 38 F7
Spey 8 E3
Spittal 16 D1
Split 16 F3
Spokane 32 C2
Spree 15 F3
Springfield (Ill., USA) 33 J4
Springfield (Mo., USA) 33 H4
Springs 28 N9
Spurn Head 6 H3
Sri Lanka 22 E7
Srinagar 22 C2
Stafford 6 E4
Stanley 37 D8
Stara Zagora 17 K3
Stargard 15 F2
Stavanger 13 E7
Stavropol' 18 D5
Stewart I. 39 M11
Stirling 8 E4
Stockholm 13 G7
Stockport 6 E3
Stockton-on-Tees 6 F2
Stoke-on-Trent 6 E3
Stonehaven 8 F4
Stonehenge 7 F5

Stornoway 8 B2
Strabane 9 D2
Strait of Dover 7 J6
Stralsund 14 E1
Stranraer 8 D6
Strasbourg 11 H2
Stratford-upon-Avon 7 F4
Stromeferry 8 C3
Stroud 7 E5
Stuttgart 14 C4
Suakin 20 C6
Subotica 17 G1
Suchow 25 J4
Sucre 36 C4
Sudan 20 B6
Sudbury 31 H7
Sudetes Mts. 15 G3
Suez 20 B3
Suez, Gulf of 20 B4
Suez Canal 20 B3
Sukkur 22 B3
Sulaiman Range 22 B3
Sulawesi 26 F6
Sulu Sea 26 E4
Sumatra 26 B6
Sumba 26 E7
Sumbawa 26 E7
Sumy 18 C4
Sunderland 6 F2
Sundsvall 13 G6
Superior, Lake 33 J2
Surabaya 26 D7
Surakarta 26 D7
Surat 22 C4
Suriname 86 D2
Sverdlovsk 18 E4
Swains I. 40 H8
Swansea 7 D5
Swatow 25 J6
Swaziland 28 P9
Sweden 13
Swindon 7 F5
Switzerland 11
Sydney (Australia) 39 J6
Sydney (Canada) 31 K7
Syktyvkar 18 D3
Syracuse 33 L3
Syr Darya 18 E5
Syria 20 C2
Syrian Desert 20 C3
Szczecin 15 F2
Szeged 15 J5
Szombathely 15 G5

T
Tabora 29 H5
Tabriz 20 E2
Tabuk 20 C4
Tacoma 32 B2
Taegu 25 L3
Taejon 25 L3
Taganrog 18 C5
Tagus 12 C3
Tahiti 41 L8
T'aichung 25 K6
T'ainan 25 K6
Taipei 25 K5
Taiwan 25 K6
Taiyuan 25 H3
Taizz 20 D7
Tajrish 21 F2
Talaud Is. 27 G5
Talca 37 B6
Talcahuano 37 B6
Tallahassee 35 H1
Tallinn 18 C4
Tamale 28 D4
Tamar 7 C6
Tambov 18 D4
Tampa 35 H2
Tampere 13 H6
Tampico 34 E3
Tamworth (Australia) 39 J6
Tamworth (England) 6 F4
Tana 13 J5
Tanga 29 H5
Tanganyika, Lake 29 G5
Tangier 28 D1
Tangshan 25 J3
Tanimbar Is. 27 H7
Tanjungkarang-Telukbetung 26 C7
Tanta 20 B3
Tanzania 29 H5
Tapachula 34 F5
Tapajós 36 D3
Tarancón 12 E2
Táranto 16 F4
Tarbert 8 B3
Tarbes 10 E5
Taree 39 J6
Tarnow 15 J3
Tarragona 12 G2
Tarrasa 12 G2
Tashkent 18 E5
Tasmania 39 H8
Tasman Sea 39 N10
Tat-ung 25 H2
Taunton 7 D5
Taupo 39 O9
Taupo, Lake 39 O9
Tauranga 39 O9
Taurus Mts. 20 B2

Tavoy 23 H6
Tawau 26 E5
Tay 8 E4
Tay, Loch 8 D4
Taymyr Peninsula 18 F2
Tbilisi 18 D5
Tees 6 F2
Tegucigalpa 34 G5
Tehran 21 F2
Teifi 7 C4
Tekirdag 17 L4
Tel-Aviv-Yafo 20 B3
Telford 6 E4
Temirtau 18 E4
Temuco 37 B6
Tennant Creek 38 E3
Tennessee 33 J4
Tennessee R. 33 J4
Tepic 34 D3
Teresina 36 E3
Terni 16 D3
Terre Adélie 43 J3
Tete 29 H6
Tetuan 28 D1
Texas 32 G5
Thailand 26 B2
Thailand, Gulf of 23 J6
Thames 7 F5
Thar Desert 22 C3
Tharthar Basin 20 D3
Thásos 17 K4
Thessaloniki 17 J4
Thimbu 23 F3
Thionville 11 H2
Thíra 17 K6
Thunder Bay 31 H7
Thuringian Forest 14 D3
Thurles 9 D4
Thurso 8 E2
Tiber 16 D3
Tibesti Mts. 29 F3
Tientsin 25 J3
Tierra del Fuego 37 C8
Tigris 20 D3
Tijuana 34 A1
Timaru 39 N10
Timbuktu 28 D3
Timisoara 17 H2
Timmins 31 H7
Timor 27 G7
Timor Sea 38 C2
Tínos 17 K6
Tipperary 9 C4
Tiranë 17 G4
Tiraspol 17 M1
Tiree 8 B4
Tirgu Mures 17 K1
Tirich Mir 21 K2
Tirso 16 B4
Tiruchirapalli 22 D6
Tisza 15 J5
Titicaca, Lake 36 C4
Titograd 17 G3
Titov Veles 17 H4
Tlemcen 28 D1
Toamasina 29 J6
Toba, Lake 26 A5
Tobruk 29 G1
Tocantins 36 E3
Togo 28 E4
Tokelau 40 H7
Tokyo 25 N3
Tolbukhin 17 L3
Toledo (Spain) 12 D3
Toledo (USA) 33 K3
Toliara 29 J7
Toluca 34 E4
Tol'yatti 18 D4
Tomsk 18 F4
Tonga 40 H8
Tonle Sap 26 B3
Toowoomba 39 J5
Topeka 33 G4
Torbay 7 D6
Töre 13 H5
Torne 13 H5
Toronto 31 J8
Torreón 34 D2
Torres Strait 27 K8
Tortosa 12 G2
Toruń 15 H2
Toulon 11 G5
Toulouse 10 E5
Tours 10 E3
Townsville 39 H3
Tralee 9 B4
Trang 26 A4
Transantarctic Mts. 43
Transylvanian Alps 17 J2
Trápani 16 D5
Trasimeno, Lake 16 D3
Trebon 15 F4
Trent 6 G3
Trenton 33 M4
Trieste 16 D2
Tríkkala 17 H5
Trincomalee 22 E7
Trinidad & Tobago 36 C1
Tripoli (Lebanon) 20 C3
Tripoli (Libya) 29 F1
Trivandrum 22 D7
Trois-Rivières 31 J7
Trollhättan 13 F7
Tromso 13 G5